ENDORSEMENTS

"I have known Christy Hill since 1992. Her heart for purity, love for Jesus, and words about God's love are unmatched. *Journey into Intimacy* is a book that will cause you to lose yourself in understanding the depths of Jesus's love for us and walking in healing of traumatic places in your life. There is no better book to have in your hands at this time."

—Cindy McGill
Author of *What Your Dreams Are Telling You,*
Words That Work, and *Methods to End the Madness*
www.cindymcgill.org

"Christy has given us a treasure that everyone needs to store up in their heart! *Journey into Intimacy* is the sacred path that every lover of God must walk. Her writings will open your soul, like a window thrown open, to the delight of God's heart over you! Take the journey, step into intimacy, and discover that it is more pleasurable than you imagined! From cover to cover, you will experience God's heart for you—unveiled and inviting you closer! Thank you, Christy Hill, for this book! Tell everyone you know to buy it, read it, then give it as a gift! You'll be glad you did!"

—Dr. Brian Simmons
Passion & Fire Ministries

JOURNEY *into* INTIMACY

JOURNEY into INTIMACY

Christy Hill

Scripture quotations marked "DARBY" are taken from the Darby Translation Bible (Public Domain).

Scripture quotations marked "KJV" are taken from the Holy Bible, King James Version (Public Domain).

Scripture quotations marked (NASB) are taken from the (NASB®) New American Standard Bible®, Copyright © 1960, 1971, 1977, 1995, 2020 by The Lockman Foundation. Used by permission. All rights reserved. lockman.org.

Scripture quotations marked (NIV) are taken from the Holy Bible, New International Version®, NIV®. Copyright © 1973, 1978, 1984, 2011 by Biblica, Inc.™ Used by permission of Zondervan. All rights reserved worldwide. www.zondervan.comThe "NIV" and "New International Version" are trademarks registered in the United States Patent and Trademark Office by Biblica, Inc.™

Scripture quotations marked (NKJV) are taken from the New King James Version®. Copyright © 1982 by Thomas Nelson. Used by permission. All rights reserved.

All Hebrew and Greek translations taken from "Strong's Exhaustive Concordance of the Bible" by James Strong. Published by Abingdon Press, 1890 (1986).

ISBN Paperback: 978-1-966462-08-8

ISBN Ebook: 978-1-961557-98-7

ISBN Hardback: 978-1-966462-09-5

Library of Congress Control Number: 2023910685

Messenger Books
30 N. Gould Ste. R
Sheridan, WY 82801

CONTENTS

PART VI

DEDICATION

With love and thanks to the man of my life,
my wonderful husband, Forrest.
My heart is safe with you.

For my children, may my ceiling be your floor.

To all who share my hunger to know the Lord, I freely offer my journey.

"And yet I show you a more excellent way."
— 1 Corinthians 12:31b, NLT —

INTRODUCTION

All my life, I have hungered for God. When I was a small child, I would watch the clouds in the summer sky and wonder when Jesus would return. I had been told He would come again, as He had once gone away through the clouds. So, I watched, trying to imagine Him riding on the sunbeams and wishing He would return – for me.

As I grew, I heard the stories of the saints and the miraculous works of God in their lives, and I wished I could experience His miracles, too. When I was a teenager, I discovered God is still doing miracles on the earth, and the experiences of the early believers recorded in the book of Acts are still happening among believers today. Oh, I felt like the kid at the back of the classroom, frantically waving her hand and saying, "Pick me, God! Pick me!"

At age 15 I was baptized in the Holy Spirit. Suddenly, Jesus became very real to me. I sensed His presence and felt His touch. We walked together day by day. I learned to recognize the voice of the Holy Spirit speaking in my heart as He taught me how to live. The Bible came alive to me. I carried it with me everywhere and shared with my friends about the amazing love of God. I prayed for healing of sickness and injuries, for help in difficult circumstances and heartaches, and I saw the Lord answer many prayers. Still, I hungered for more.

Several years later, when I was a young wife and mother, a friend introduced me to the Song of Solomon. I had never looked into the Song before. The book was a mystery to me, beautiful poetry, yet so obscure. But I will never forget the way I felt that day; it was as if someone had opened a door in a tall garden wall, and I had stepped into a vast and verdant place just beckoning me to explore.

From where I stood on the threshold of this sunlit garden, I could see groves of fruit trees and gently flowing streams, soft, grassy valleys, and snow-capped peaks. I never wanted to leave it. I wanted to run and twirl, to eat the fruit and lie in the grass. I wanted to stay – to learn all the secrets the garden had to tell me about the heart of God.

For more than 40 years, I have walked in this garden with the Lord. The poetic images of the Song have become keys that have unlocked treasures in the heart of God for me. I go to the Song when I'm hungry for God and find a feast laid out to freely enjoy. I go again the very next day and find the feast is new. I never tire of the beauty. I have yet to come to the end of what it has to teach me.

Studying the Song has changed me. It has shown me what God's heart is like, and I know I will never be the same. I have experienced His tenderness and His compassion. I have learned about forgiveness and have been taught His redemption. I have seen the honor in His eyes as He turned them upon me, and I've wept as I glimpsed the value He places upon my life.

I have learned He does not want a marriage of convenience. He is a passionate God. He desires oneness with His bride. I still tremble as I join Him in the place where He has led me. I am learning to take my place – seated with Him, even on His throne. But I am getting ahead of myself. I will show you. Please, will you come with me into this book and let me share my treasures with you? I promise you the door stands wide, and Jesus beckons to you.

How can I be sure? I saw your reflection when I looked into His eyes. His eyes, gentle beyond measure, are looking at you even now. He knows your name. He has loved you all your life. He has kept you for this time and place and put this book into your hand. This is not happenstance. You are His beloved and He wants you to know how He loves you.

Before I begin our study in the Song, I would like to share with you a vision I once had of the Scriptures.

I saw an open Bible. At first the words looked like two-dimensional print on a page, then suddenly they took on great depth. The printed words had changed. They now looked as if they were in the sky, in space, and there was no paper binding them. As I watched, I saw each word become a doorway, an invitation for me to step through into a vast place. Each word or phrase became a portal that could usher me into a revelation of the Infinite One.

I have learned to study the Bible in this way. I approach it as if the words are doorways into the mysteries of God. When I look at the words in this way, they become living portraits of His face. They become visions of His kindness that reveal His heart.

I study to know God, to see the smile in His eyes, to feel His nearness, even His breath upon me. These are the mysteries that are ours to discover. I pray that as we look together into the Song, you will come with me and find your home within these words: "I am His treasure, and He has given Himself to me."

The Song of Solomon is an allegory that tells the story of the bride of Christ on the earth as she is lifted out of fear and oppression and enters her new life with the king. The bride of Christ is made up of individuals, each as precious to Him as the other. We come to Him as individuals, and together, make up His corporate bride, His church. The Song of Solomon follows the church as she discovers the truths that transform her, causing her to become the bride: a consort made ready for her king.

But the Song of Solomon is also the story of the Bridegroom as He seeks and woos His bride. He does not leave us alone to struggle through life while we attempt to become the bride prepared for her Bridegroom. His Spirit is here with us, loving us, helping us every step of the way. This is the story of the Lord's heart for His bride. We will see His heart in amazing clarity.

Based upon my first introduction to the Song of Solomon in the beautiful work, *Union and Communion with Christ,* by J. Hudson Taylor, we will study the Song as a story divided into six sections. Each section takes the bride more deeply into the heart of God. Not all the story is hearts and flowers. There is doubt, fear, confusion, guilt, shame . . . It is my story – and yours. It is humanity's story – and God's. Let us begin.

PART I

SONG OF SOLOMON 1:1 – 2:7, NKJV

The song of songs, which is Solomon's.
Let him kiss me with the kisses of his mouth—
For your love is better than wine.
Because of the fragrance of your good ointments,
Your name is ointment poured forth;
Therefore the virgins love you.
Draw me away!
We will run after you.
The king has brought me into his chambers.
We will be glad and rejoice in you.
We will remember your love more than wine.
Rightly do they love you.
I am dark, but lovely,
O daughters of Jerusalem,
Like the tents of Kedar,
Like the curtains of Solomon.
Do not look upon me, because I am dark,
Because the sun has tanned me.
My mother's sons were angry with me;

They made me the keeper of the vineyards,
But my own vineyard I have not kept.
Tell me, O you whom I love,
Where you feed your flock,
Where you make it rest at noon.
For why should I be as one who veils herself
By the flocks of your companions?

If you do not know, O fairest among women,
Follow in the footsteps of the flock,
And feed your little goats
Beside the shepherds' tents.
I have compared you, my love,
To my filly among Pharaoh's chariots.
Your cheeks are lovely with ornaments,
Your neck with chains of gold.
We will make you ornaments of gold
With studs of silver.

While the king is at his table,
My spikenard sends forth its fragrance.
A bundle of myrrh is my beloved to me
That lies all night between my breasts.
My beloved is to me a cluster of henna blooms
In the vineyards of En Gedi.

Behold, you are fair, my love!
Behold, you are fair!
You have dove's eyes.

Behold, you are handsome, my beloved!
Yes, pleasant!
Also our bed is green.
The beams of our houses are cedar,
And our rafters of fir.

I am the rose of Sharon,
And the lily of the valleys.

Like a lily among thorns,
So is my love among the daughters.

Like an apple tree among the trees of the woods,
So is my beloved among the sons.
I sat down in his shade with great delight,
And his fruit was sweet to my taste.
He brought me to the banqueting house,
And his banner over me was love.
Sustain me with cakes of raisins,
Refresh me with apples,
For I am lovesick.
His left hand is under my head,
And his right hand embraces me.
I charge you, O daughters of Jerusalem,
By the gazelles or by the does of the field,
Do not stir up nor awaken love
Until it pleases.

AWAKENING

"The Song of Songs, which is Solomon's" (Song 1:1).

"Song of songs," like the phrase "heart of hearts," speaks of the ultimate: the most, or deepest, or highest. This song is the song of God's heart. It is the revelation that will bring us into the treasured place the Apostle John enjoyed. In it we learn how to lean against Jesus' breast and listen to His heartbeat. This is where we find God's pulse; where His blood runs sure, and strong, and unending; and in it we discover how to enter His rest.

Solomon's name comes from the Hebrew word "shalom," which is translated "peace." It also means: well, happy, safe, sound, tranquil, in health, rest, harmony, and prosperity. The word embodies the idea of well-being on every level of human experience. Well-being: so elusive, so pursued.

"The Song of Songs, which is Solomon's." The Prince of Peace is singing His song over you now. You have heard His song before, though perhaps you didn't recognize it. He sang it in the breeze that carried the scent of rain. He was singing among the stars when you stopped to marvel at their light. He was telling you He loved you when the flowers began to bloom. He spoke peace to you when stormy winds whipped about you. He comforted you when you cried out in fear. His peace belongs to you. It is your home, your place of residence. The door is standing open before you, inviting you to enter into the goodness He has readied for you. *Come with me . . .*

The journey begins with the bride saying, "Let him kiss me with the kisses of his mouth" (Song 1:2). She enters his presence through this door, and so must each of us if we will follow there. Upon the doorway into our Bridegroom's heartbeat are written the words, "let Him." How little we want to let Him, and how impossible it is for us to go on until we do. I have spent many months meditating on these two simple words, "let Him," and oh, how I have wrestled with them.

I wanted to bring to God the best in me, but I found the best in me unworthy of an offering to someone so fine. I wanted to prepare my heart in goodness so it could become a gift He would be pleased to receive. For a long time, I tried to make myself good, but with each struggle to bring my heart into line with the love of God, with each time I sought to escape the selfishness that is in me, with each attempt to hide from the pride and deny the guilt, I heard Jesus say, "Let me! Let me kiss you with the kisses of my mouth, and these things will lose their hold."

1 John 4:19 (NIV) says, "We love because He first loved us." We do not begin by doing. We do not begin by giving. We cannot walk. We cannot serve. We cannot even love until we have received. We must begin by "letting Him."

This is a very difficult thing to do. To "let Him kiss me" requires that I be still and receive His love. It demands that I humbly take in His words of endearment. It requires discipline and determination to receive the love He wants to give. To "let Him" requires me to cultivate the attitude that what God wants to give to me takes precedence over my estimation of my own worthiness.

We cannot insist to God that we are unworthy of His love and affection if we are to cross the threshold into intimacy with Him. We have to tell our souls to be quiet. We have to determine within our hearts to be open and receptive to His love. This is not about our worthiness. This is all about God's desire to give His love to us.

Do you want to bless God? Do you want to do something that will cause His heart to swell with joy? Let Him kiss you. That is, let Him tell you how He loves you, and do not turn away. Do not limit what He may say. Do not deflect it, or qualify it, or attribute it to others. Let Him kiss you with the kisses of His mouth. Let His words go into your heart and rest there. Receive His words. Let your heart be fertile soil for the seeds of His words that they may take root, and spring up, and bear fruit.

I promise you won't become proud by receiving and believing the things God says to you. I have found, much to my surprise, rather than becoming prideful at the words of my Lord, I am deeply aware of my absolute dependence upon Him in all He says about me. To be who God says I am requires a consistent and deliberate dependence upon Him; this protects my heart from selfish attitudes which would separate me from Him.

The next words of the bride are turned toward her Bridegroom: "For your love is better than wine."

Psalms 104:15 (NKJV) tells us, ". . . [W]ine . . . makes glad the heart of man." Wine has the ability to soothe and relax, to warm people, and to make them feel happy. It is a drink used to celebrate special occasions and to enhance the taste of fine foods.

The bride has received the kisses of her bridegroom and he has captured her attention. Now, instead of speaking about him, she turns toward him and tells him his love is better than wine. She feels giddy at this first taste of his love. He has made her feel hopeful; something she had not felt before. Her life has suddenly taken on a new texture. She no longer sees her future stretching before her merely recreating her unhappy past. His love has cut across the sameness and the sadness of her life. He offers her a joyous alternative.

She says, "Your love makes me happier and more content than I have ever been before." These are the words of the first blush of a love that will soon come to be a passionate flame in her heart. The bridegroom's love for his bride is teaching her to open her heart to him. But although she is thrilled and intrigued by this unexpected welcome, she has not even begun to understand the extent of his commitment to her.

FRAGRANCE

In my hometown in eastern Oregon, an elusive scent floats in the spring breezes, which fills me with wonder. As a child I sometimes caught it in fleeting breaths and would pause to fill my lungs in utter delight. It was a delicate fragrance and was present for only a short time. As the fragrance appeared each successive spring, I began to recognize it as one I had known before and of which I wanted more. It was many years before I found it was the locust trees in bloom which produced that wonderful smell. When I discovered the source of that lovely scent, I ever afterward wanted to live in a place where there are locust trees, so that during those few days every spring I might again experience the pleasure of their fragrance.

There is something mysterious about fragrance. It can be elusive and fleeting, yet, with a brief touch, it has the power to awaken in us a longing for something we may not be able to express or identify. Fragrance has a drawing power. Who of us is able to pass a rose without burying our faces in its petals? Fragrance awakens our hunger, offering the promise of something more, and fragrance touches our memories as no other stimulus can. When we catch a scent of bygone times, suddenly we remember long forgotten scenes, faces, and feelings.

Fragrance awakens our hearts and calls to us to seek its source. In Kenneth Grahame's children's classic, *The Wind in the Willows*, Mole, having been gone from his home for a long time while on adventures with Rat and Toad, one evening sniffs the air, changes his course, and heads for home. Rat finds him and asks him where he is going, to which Mole replies he is going home because, he says, "I smelt it . . . and I wanted it."[1]

There is something in God I have sensed, something as indefinable as fragrance. Like Mole, I have smelled it, and I want it. And like Mole, at times, all I have to lead me is a seemingly elusive scent. And yet – the Spirit of God is the breath of God. Breath carries fragrance. It is by the breath of God that we are drawn to seek the source of a fragrance so lovely it is without compare.

Like my locust blossoms, we may spend many years with brief and infrequent awareness of the fragrance of God's presence, yet the memory of it is so sweet we are drawn to it with great longing. Unlike my locust blossoms, the source of this fragrance does not appear for only a few days and then disappear. This fragrance is found in something so sure that once we find the source of it we can live there for the rest of our lives if we choose.

"Because of the fragrance of your good ointments." The word "good" here is repeated in Hebrew in its plural form. I don't believe that this emphasis makes his ointments doubly good. I believe it is exponential, like the "seventy times seven" in Jesus' teaching on forgiveness (Matthew 18:22, NKJV), or like "one chase(d) a thousand, and two put ten thousand to flight" in the Song of Moses (Deuteronomy 32:30,

NKJV). His ointments are good *times* good. I believe you could say they are infinitely good. But what is this ointment?

"Your name is ointment poured forth." In Hebrew culture, a name describes the substance of a person, often referring to something about their character or nature. In this little verse we find a portal into a place so vast in God that after years of looking into it I have never glimpsed its borders.

There is a great deal I could say here, but I will leave it with this: our God and Father has given us many names by which to call Him, and every one of them carries a promise with it. In every name of God, I have found Him offering me something of Himself to be known and explored. Every word God uses to describe Himself is a word we can call on when we have need. It is as if He has said, "What do you need?" Once we identify the need, He answers, "I will supply it in myself," then gives us a name by which to call Him.

The most fascinating thing to me about this whole exchange is that we are designed by our creator to be filled by Him in every part of our being, but He leaves it to us in our free will to discover our need of Him and give Him entrance. He doesn't invade us. He leads us to discover Him and give place to Him as we gain understanding of our own frailties.

Ointment or fragrant oil is a symbol throughout Scripture of the presence and work of the Holy Spirit in relation to mankind. Anointing with oil speaks of the work of the Spirit of Grace upon our lives. I use the term "Spirit of Grace" not because it is a pretty phrase, but because of the particular meaning of the word "grace." Many people interchange "grace" with "mercy" and can see little difference between the two. But I believe while it is true that grace includes the mercy of God, it has a much more far-reaching meaning.

Mercy speaks of the gift of love and forgiveness that we do not deserve and can never earn, but that belongs to us in Jesus. But grace is the substance of the presence of God that gives us the ability to do those things only God can do in and through us. To speak of the Holy Spirit as the Spirit of Grace is to refer to the enabling presence of the member of the Godhead who brooded over the surface of the deep and caused order to come out of chaos at the word of the Lord.

The clearest picture I have ever had of the work of grace in a life is an illustration the Lord gave to me as I prayed for a friend one day. My friend was going through a very difficult time, and I asked the Lord to give her the help she needed to overcome in her situation. As I prayed, the Lord gave me a picture of my friend climbing a rock cliff. She was very high on the cliff and still had a distance to go before she reached the top. She was small and weak and had climbed a long way. As I asked the Lord for grace for her, I saw the substance of God go into her. Working within and through her, His power gave her the ability to find the next hand and footholds as well as the strength to lift herself up to the next level. Step-by-step, He supplied strength and wisdom to her to move through that perilous place.

What I saw was not an external application of God's hand to move my friend along, nor a sovereign work of His apart from her. It was the substance of His being poured into her, working in and through her, to help her do the thing that would have been impossible for her apart from Him. This is grace. The Spirit of Grace is the one who pours out on us like oil, anointing us to do those things only God can do. By Him we are given all that is available to us in every name of God. "Your Name is ointment poured forth."

ENTREATY

The bridegroom's goodness has begun to open the eyes of his beloved. She looks around and sees there are those who have already known the sweetness of his fellowship. And she says, "Therefore the virgins love you" (Song 1:3).

Virgins are young, unmarried women. They represent people who have not entangled themselves in worldly lifestyles. They are unattached in the sense that the lures of fortune, prestige, and comforts apart from God have not captured their hearts. The bride sees in the virgins a singleness of vision she is beginning to understand and to desire.

As a result, the bride calls out to her bridegroom, "Draw me away!" (Song 1:4). That she asks him to draw her indicates she realizes she does not trust her ability to go to him on her own. She has tasted of something that has whetted her appetite for more and she wants him to take her on.

"Draw me away" is a prayer of my heart that has taken many forms through the years I have walked with Jesus. There have been times of great eloquence in my journals when I have asked for His presence to captivate my heart and cause me to come into agreement with Him for the things that are in His heart for me. And there have been times when I was so undone, all I had the ability to say was "baa" like the helpless lamb caught in the briers I felt myself to be.

Many times, I have felt like the child of my friend who used to say to her daddy, "Tum det me!" (Come get me.) And as silly as it sounds, I cried out to my Father with those very words on the occasions when my helplessness threatened to overwhelm me. "Tum det me!" Draw me away. The wonderful thing about this is the Lord has never failed to answer this cry of my heart. Whenever I have asked Him to pick me up, to take me on, to rescue me, He has always come.

But this drawing away isn't only a cry to be rescued or brought to even ground; I believe there is a hunger that God has put into each of our hearts – a yearning only He can satisfy. I have come to understand that with every desire to draw nearer to Him, there is an invitation from our God to explore, discover, and be satisfied in Him. "Draw me away!" are the bride's words. But I believe she is echoing her bridegroom's heart's cry, "Come to me!"

Yes, Lord, take us deeper. Take us on this journey
into the mysteries of your heart. Don't allow us to settle
in the shallows in our knowledge of you. You are Infinite God! Cause
us to hunger and thirst for more. Cause us to come into agreement
with you for all that is in your heart for each of us. There is no ceiling
on our lives. The only limitation in our exploration of you is our own
desire to pursue you for more. You delight in the pursuit and in the
giving of yourself to those who seek you. You delight in us and in
drawing us nearer to the source of your heartbeat. Come get us, Lord,
and take us away! We want to be with you where you are. We want to
lean our heads against your breast and listen until our hearts come

into rhythm with your own. Draw us away, Lord, from all of the distractions of daily life and lead us into the stillness. Cause us to rest in the secret place with you.

DRAWING NEAR

"We will run after you" (Song 1:4).

The virgins also express their desire to follow after the bridegroom, so attractive is he. Yet, it is the bride alone who can say, "The king has brought me into his chambers" (Song 1:4).

The first introduction of the bride into intimacy with her bridegroom has her overcome by his grandeur. She is very aware the man she has married is a man to be reckoned with. He is the king; and to her amazement, he has chosen her for his bride.

In the same way, it is right for us to be overcome by the majesty of our Lord. It is right that we bow before Him in honor and praise. It is correct to see the awesome splendor and glory of our God, and to worship Him as our creator and our redeemer. But we are not merely the created and redeemed of the Most High. As wonderful as these appellations are, as we learn to apply them to ourselves and begin to enjoy the freedom that is inherent to us in them, we are not to stop there. God has called us to a place far beyond the glory we enjoy as

His created and redeemed. We are His beloved, and as such we have been brought wondering, often disbelieving, into the chamber of our king, our Bridegroom.

The first time I saw the Lord high and lifted up upon His throne, I was little more than a child. I saw a golden stairway through the clouds leading up to a very large throne. I remember the awe I felt at this first glimpse of His glory. I stood at the bottom of the stairway gazing up with longing at the person on the throne. I remember that I felt unsure, overwhelmed, inadequate – yet I longed to draw near, so I began to climb. Step by step I went up the stairs, passing angelic persons on the way. When I reached the top I did not stop, I continued to climb until I was seated in the very lap of the one who loved me.

As I look at that vision from the distance of more than fifty years, I wonder at my audacity at climbing into the lap of God. He was seated in majesty. He was surrounded by heavenly beings. He was high and lifted up. Why did I think I could join Him there?

The only answer I can give to this is that I was responding to what was in His heart. I was the child to whom her Father, the King, had opened His arms. Climbing into His lap at that moment was appropriate because it was what He wanted me to do. This is the way we enter the chambers of the King. We draw near in response to the irresistible longing reaching out to us from His own heart. "The King has brought me into His chambers."

"We will be glad and rejoice in you," the virgins say to the bride (Song 1:4). They are happy in her marriage.

The union of the bride with the king gives cause for rejoicing to all around. We find a picture of this in the story of Esther; when righteous Mordecai was in the place of authority the people rejoiced, but when wicked Haman was the one advising the king and manipulating the laws toward his evil bent, all of the people were in confusion.

Proverbs 29:2 (NKJV) tells us, "When the righteous are in authority, the people rejoice; but when a wicked man rules, the people groan."

When those who have drawn near to the King live as His among those who haven't known Him, the atmosphere of His kingdom rule is present with them. The peace and joy of His presence flows through their lives and brings blessing to all within their scope of influence.

LOVELY

To the bridegroom, the women say,
"We will remember your love more than wine" (Song 1:4).

The bride sees the rightness in this. The king is worthy to be loved. He is someone to whom honor is due, not merely by rank or position, but because he is generous, compassionate, and kind. So, she says to her bridegroom, "Rightly do they love you."

But, regarding herself she says, "I am dark" (Song 1:5).

"But lovely," her bridegroom answers.

"O daughters of Jerusalem," she continues, "I am like the tents of Kedar" (Kedar refers to the black goat hair tents of the shepherds).

"Like the (embroidered linen) curtains of Solomon," insists her bridegroom.

Then in shame over her condition that has become very clear to her in contrast to the glory of her king, the bride says to her bridegroom,

"Do not look upon me, because I am dark, because the sun has tanned me" (Song 1:6).

Part of Psalm 46:10 (NIV) entreats us, "Be still, and know I am God." Stillness and knowing go hand in hand. "To know" is to be intimately acquainted. It is the word used to describe the physical intimacy between a man and his wife. It is a word that indicates a union that is for both parties a giving and receiving, a commingling of heart and soul.

It was with great wonder I began to approach the idea of being joined to God in such a way. When at first the idea came, in mortification, I rejected it. But the gentle fluttering in my spirit persisted. The same voice I had come to know and trust as the one who knows me best brought me back to this idea again and again until I was forced to ask Him to teach me what He meant by it.

Little by little, and with infinite tenderness, He taught me to allow Him to give His heart to me. He coaxed my heart open with His acceptance of me. In response I learned to give my own heart to Him with greater abandon and deeper trust.

Many times, when I have been overcome with shame and sorrow at the wrong things within me, I have tried to hide, but I cannot hide for long from the one who loves me. He finds me; then, seeing all, He gathers me to Himself, quieting my fears.

"Lord, I'm so sorry," I begin.

"Hush. Be still," He says, not allowing me to follow the downward path into self-recrimination. He knows all that is in my heart, and instead of allowing me to flog myself in penance, He entreats me to be still and receive His love and acceptance. "Be still, and know I am."

"But I am dark."

"You are lovely."

You are lovely. Please, dear friend, let your heart receive these words in the way the thirsty land takes in the rain. Drink of them as much as you are able. Allow them to soften the hard and crusty places of your heart.

We all come to God bearing the wounds of life. We come bringing memories of what we have done and of what has been done to us. We learn to cope with life, and our hearts become scarred and calloused. When presented with words such as these, it is natural to reject them.

We say to God, "You cannot say this about me. I *know* what I have done. I am dark." Yet He invariably responds, "But I know you better, and you are lovely in my eyes."

Only by returning to drink in these words repeatedly over time will we be able to enter into agreement with them. Agreement with God's assessment of us is what He is looking for from us. Do not be discouraged if it takes time but allow me to encourage you to take a sip of this cup of the water of life being held before you today.

You are lovely – lovely to God. He sees you – and He says you are lovely. How can this be? You will come to see, but for now do not try to understand. Just receive.

ACCEPTED

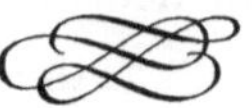

> "My mother's sons were angry with me;
> they made me the keeper of the vineyards,
> but my own vineyard I have not kept" (Song 1:6).

In her bridegroom the bride has found an acceptance she has never before known. In the past, her days were filled with the struggle to appease the careless and cruel people who ruled her life. Her mother's sons were never satisfied. But in her bridegroom, she has found one who looks upon her flaws and sees beauty.

"Mother's sons" refers to the religious authority that requires her behavior to align with accepted norms. Keeping the vineyards speaks of the duties associated with trying to satisfy her conscience and gain the approval of the religious people in her life. Despite her striving to please, she is aware of her personal bankruptcy. "My own vineyard I have not kept."

I, too, spent many years under a religious system, striving with all that was in me to meet the standards which would appease my conscience and please my god. I thought I was serving the God of the Universe. I didn't understand I was following a path of servitude into a lifeless place. My speech was filled with "I'm sorrys." My soul was filled with guilt. Not only did I spend all of my strength striving to be a good person, but I also tried to lay my impossible standards on those within my scope of influence – until Jesus came and rescued me.

There came a night when God allowed me to feel the crushing heaviness of the religious system I was trying so hard to appease. I lay on the floor and wept as the impossible weight pressed me down. Then Jesus came to me, lifted it away, and showed me that all He had ever wanted was to give Himself to me. It took many weeks for me to understand nothing was required of me that He didn't first provide.

I struggled to agree with Him in this new place. It was such a foreign thought to not have to strive in my relationship with Him. I kept trying to bring to Him what I thought He would require. I tried to offer prayers. I tried to give Him praise. But He impressed upon me that even my prayers and my worship must first spring from Him.

When at last I began to agree to let go of what I had believed was required of me, an amazing thing happened: The Holy Spirit began to pour into me in a powerful way. He gave me prayer that carried such an anointing I knew it would accomplish the purposes of God. I learned to enter into worship by coming into the stillness with Jesus and waiting for His breath. Now I wait for the Holy Spirit to come and lift me into worship. I have come to believe this is what it means to offer holy praise to God.

FOLLOWING

The bride has found in her beloved one whose acceptance
is so sweet she wants to spend every moment of the day with him.
"Tell me, O you whom I love, where you feed your flock, where you
make it rest at noon. For why should I be as one who veils
herself by the flocks of your companions?" (Song 1:7).

She is asking, "Where will I find you in the light of day? I want to be with you in your work. Must I remain separated from you while others walk beside you through the day, and I am left with their accounts of your doings?" No longer content with having a secondhand knowledge of the activities of her bridegroom, the bride now seeks how she may join him.

The bridegroom answers, "If you do not know, O fairest among women, follow in the footsteps of the flock, and feed your little goats beside the shepherds' tents" (Song 1:8).

The bridegroom instructs his love that she will find the answer to her questions by following the path others have gone before. But she must follow those who have found him, and she must stay with those who can impart their knowledge to her.

Many and varied are the pictures in the Song used to describe the relationship between the bride and bridegroom. This passage speaks of shepherding. The bride sees her king as a shepherd. Do you find it curious the king spends his days herding sheep? Yet we know Jesus described Himself as the Good Shepherd.

The bride doesn't want to be separated from him in her day-to-day activities but yearns to be with him throughout the day. I, too, want all my life to be spent in the presence of Jesus. Any time spent apart from Him is wasted. I don't want to suffer the loss of even a moment in His presence.

I find it intriguing that he instructs his bride that the way to find him is by following in the footprints of the flock, and to learn his ways she must remain beside the shepherds' tents. Here is a royal person being instructed to stay near and follow the shepherds. Shepherds were not exalted among men. Like the farmers and ranchers of my acquaintance, they were unpretentious, hard-working people. Yet who better to show the bride how to find her bridegroom than one who has learned to care for sheep?

Many years ago, when I was a young woman full of zeal, I had a great desire to do important things. I wanted to be involved in ministry. I wanted to go to Bible college. I wanted to help pastor a church. I wanted to make a difference in people's lives and in the world. But instead of Bible school, my husband and I settled into marriage and making a living. We understood God was leading us in the way we were going. Ministry would surely come later.

I became a mother, and my life was filled with the care of our children. I continued to hope I would get to do important things for the Lord, but for years the only songs I sang were lullabies, and instead of speaking with adults about deep biblical truths, I read Bible stories to my toddlers. Days spent wiping noses and sweeping up crumbs wasn't exactly the exciting ministry I was looking for, but when I asked the Lord where my ministry was, He assured me that if I gave my whole heart to kissing away tears and reading bedtime stories, I would be with Him in what He was doing in my life.

Eventually I learned what the bride is being given to discover. The life of a shepherd is not glamorous, nor is it very often exciting. Like the daily life of a mother, a shepherd gives his strength to care for those who cannot care for themselves. It can be exhausting and at times confusing, frustrating, and lonely, but the life of a shepherd is the choice of our Lord.

As a mother I came to know the Lord in His faithfulness, His unfailing tenderness, and His wisdom as I lived a life that was often tedious, tiring, and solitary. As I gave myself to my children, I found Jesus present with me, supplying to me the heart of a mother-shepherdess to do His work through me. I learned that to do the thing in front of me with all the love within me was to do the work of the Lord.

So, it is. Whatever pursuits our lives may hold, when we come to Jesus for grace to be faithful in tedium; when we quiet our hearts and wait until His patience fills us for the immaturity of others; when we give place to His kindness despite our fatigue; when we pour out love and strength willingly, joyfully, and would do it all again for the sheer joy of loving; this is when we have come to the place where the Shepherd feeds His flock. There we will find a place of quiet rest; a place to be still in the midst of activity. There we will be filled with His goodness when our own is gone. And in this place, we will receive the soothing balm of a heart joined to ours in deep understanding of the struggle and cost of giving and loving.

PROMISE

"I have compared you, my love, to my filly
among Pharaoh's chariots" (Song 1:9).

I believe the filly referred to by King Solomon in this passage is the horse mentioned in 2 Chronicles 1:17 that was imported from Egypt at great cost along with a very valuable chariot. For those who are looking for the application to our lives, there is a beautiful picture here.

What would it mean to you to hear the Lord say He sees in you such promise that He would give dearly to have you in His life? Most of the people I know would struggle to accept it, yet this is precisely what we can take from this passage. Most of us have allowed ourselves to believe the Lord loves us and wants us to spend eternity with Him. But this passage is about something that goes beyond a general belief in the kindness of our Savior and the goodness of our God.

The horse the king is referring to is a filly or a young mare. She is untried. She has not proven herself in battle, in tests of speed, or in feats of endurance, but the king has given a great sum for her. He sees in her something worth having, something worthy of spending his wealth to gain.

Didn't Jesus also say the kingdom of heaven is like a merchant who found a pearl of great price and gave all he had to gain it? (Matthew 13:45-46). I have always thought the bride is the pearl, Father is the merchant, and Jesus is the treasure He gave to gain the pearl. Here is a picture of wealth given to gain a treasure unseen, yet loved and wanted and highly valued by Him.

But why? Is God so blind He cannot see our deficiencies? Why does He insist there is something within us that is worthy of His interest? The king has likened his bride to his filly, saying he sees within her the promise of amazing abilities. He looks at her, sees the potential within her, and his heart is filled with joyful anticipation.

In the same way the king holds the expectation of his horse becoming a champion to in every way out-distance his adversaries, our Bride-groom sees a promise within His bride that she will bring honor to Him. Like the Proverbs 31 woman, "She does him good and not evil all the days of her life" (Proverbs 31:12, NKJV).

Why does God say this about us? I certainly can't promise to do Him good and not evil all of my life. At least it hasn't happened so far. And when I look within myself, I don't see much hope of being a champion. Yet there is something He has taught me as I've struggled within myself. He has taught me to ask Him to tell me what He sees in me. When I ask the Lord what He sees in me, I am often surprised by the twinkle in His eye as I hear Him say, "I know what I am capable of doing in your life."

He sees how He has made us, and He has taken upon Himself the weight of bringing the promise within us to light. We draw nearer to His heartbeat through the light of the hope in His eyes. The look He bends upon us, so full of confident expectation, causes us to dare to take another step toward the person He says we can be, another step deeper into intimacy.

ORNAMENTS

"Your cheeks are lovely with ornaments,
your neck with chains of gold.
We will make you ornaments of gold
with studs of silver" (Song 1:10-11).

I love this passage for what it says, but also for what it doesn't say.

There were three precious metals used in the articles for the tabernacle that Moses made. (The tabernacle was the meeting place where God dwelt with the children of Israel in the wilderness). The three metals were gold, silver, and bronze. Each of these metals carries a symbolic meaning that is unique from the others. Gold speaks of holiness, silver of redemption, and bronze of judgment.

In the tabernacle the priests were instructed to wash in the bronze laver before performing their priestly duties. The laver, or fountain, was made from articles of bronze that had been highly polished and were used to reflect the images of those who looked into them. In other words, it was made of mirrors.

As the priests began their duties, they were reminded of their own image so as not to forget their need of Him. The mirrors reflected their sinfulness and showed them the judgment that was upon their lives. The laver is a symbol of Jesus and of the cleansing that is available to us as we come to Him. He has taken all the judgment upon Himself and has washed all of our sin away.

It is difficult to take in, but the place of judgment became the scene of justice. Once the priests had washed in the laver, they were clean and free to enter the presence of God. Justice had been satisfied, and there was no longer any guilt upon them.

We are very good at remembering our sinfulness in the presence of the Lord. We hold the mirror up and tell Him what we see in our hearts, as though we are draped in bronze. It is human nature, I suppose, to identify what we are naturally, and to insist that is who we are — never mind that we have been washed in the blood of the Lamb.

Yet here we see the bride is not adorned in bronze. Her jewelry is gold and silver. We will talk of the beautiful picture of the gold in a moment; but first, I wish you will come with me for a few minutes through the door marked "studs of silver."

In the biblical world silver was chiefly used as currency. In Exodus 30, each person, old or young, rich or poor, was to bring one half-shekel of silver as the price of their redemption. No one was to bring more. No one was to bring less. Silver is the precious metal used to redeem a soul enslaved.

Jesus was betrayed for thirty pieces of silver. Thirty silver shekels were given for the life of our Lord. At one half-shekel apiece, thirty is the redemption price for sixty men. Or is it for sixty men only?

Sixty is six times ten. In biblical imagery six is the number of man and ten is the number of the law; therefore, Jesus was sold for the price of the redemption of mankind from the judgment of the law. Jesus fulfilled all of the requirements of the law and bought our freedom when he hung upon the cross. Nails pierced His hands and feet, but silver studs adorn His bride—the gift of life bought by His death.

Listed in the much-loved passage, Isaiah 53:4-5 (NKJV), are the areas of human loss that have been covered by the work of the cross: "He has borne our griefs and carried our sorrows . . . He was wounded for our transgressions, He was bruised for our iniquities; the chastisement for our peace was upon Him, and by His stripes we are healed."

Freedom from sin is central to the cross, but He also bought relief from emotional pain and mental anguish. He won both peace and health for us. Everything we have ever needed to be free to enjoy life is included in the work of the silver studs.

Gladly, our Bridegroom offers us ornaments of gold with studs of silver. Joyfully, He offers us freedom from all that holds us bound. Silver studs are ours to take, to wear in acceptance of the redemption of our lives from the bondage of our fallen state. There is no penance, nor personal sacrifice that can buy this freedom for us. It is the gift of our Lord and can only be enjoyed as such.

We have the privilege of being in a position to give our Bridegroom the joy of seeing His beloved wearing silver studs won by Him at such great cost. I am adorned in ornaments of gold with studs of silver when I accept this truth: neither sin nor failing in my past or present is able to keep me from drawing near to the one who loves me.

"We will make you ornaments of gold" (Song 1:11). Gold is the purest of metals; the most precious, the most valuable. Gold speaks to us of the holiness of God.

Holiness is unique to God. He alone is intrinsically holy. His holiness is His goodness and purity, His integrity and righteousness, His justice, truth, kindness, and love. Holiness contains all of the attributes of God which belong to Him alone. His holiness is beautiful and awe-inspiring.

In Revelation 4:8b (NKJV), we find the angels and cherubim worshiping the Lord in His holiness. They do not rest, but cry out day and night, "Holy, holy, holy, Lord God Almighty, Who was and is and is to come!" Yet in Leviticus 19:2b (NKJV), we find the Lord telling Moses to say to the people, "You shall be holy, for I the LORD your God *am* holy."

What? Did God say the people who belong to Him will be holy because He is? Surely, He just meant we would be good, or kind, or loving, or just, or righteous. I mean, we could try to be those things and achieve a measure of success at them. But be holy? Isn't God the only one who is holy? That is the wonder. He said, "I will make you ornaments of gold." He gives His holiness to us.

We actually see this in other places in the Bible. One example is the Ark of the Covenant that is made of wood (grown up of the earth) and covered in gold (holiness). It is a picture of Jesus; but as He is the first-born of many brethren, we are included in it. God has put us into Christ, so we now enjoy all the goodness that belongs to Him.

There is a reason for this, as astonishing as it may be. God gives His holiness to us *because* He is holy. Only that which is holy can be with Him. He wants us with Him. He wants us to be able to come into the secret place of His heart and be joined to Him. We cannot go there unless we are like Him, and we cannot be like Him unless He gives us His holiness.

Psalm 93 (NKJV) begins: "The Lord reigns, He is clothed in majesty;" (v.1), and ends, "Holiness adorns your house," (v.5). We are the temple of the living God. Holiness is our adornment.

The two precious metals together speak of the way God views us. In the silver, we are chosen and sought out. In the gold, we are adorned in His likeness and made abundantly suitable to be His bride. Adorned in silver and gold, we can enjoy unrestricted access to His presence. It is His great delight to give us all He is, to join us to Himself, and to share His life with us.

LOVE'S FRAGRANCE

"While the king is at his table,
my spikenard sends forth its fragrance" (Song 1:12).

ere we come to a prophetic foretelling of an amazing event.

But first I must talk about the spikenard. Spikenard is an aromatic ointment made from the roots and stems of the nard plant that grows on the slopes of the Himalayan Mountains. It is called spikenard partly because of the shape of the plant and from the derivative of "spike" from Sanskrit, which means "pure;" thus, it is pure nard. The perfume is very rare and very valuable. In the biblical world it was kept in vases of carved alabaster. There are only four passages in the Bible which speak of spikenard: two in the Song of Solomon, and two in the gospels (both of which refer to the same event).

Spikenard is unique in that out of all the spices and plants mentioned in Scripture for use in cosmetics, anointing oil, incense, and medicine, it is never included in the combinations. When we study the uses of cinnamon, frankincense, myrrh, calamus, henna, aloes, and cassia, we find they are used by the Lord to reference something of His nature that He gives to us. It may be something we offer back to Him, like the incense of our worship, but it first comes from Him – in the way our prayers ascend as the Holy Spirit intercedes through us.

Spikenard belongs to the bride alone. The Lord doesn't use it in any of His combinations of oils. He doesn't require it to be in the incense prepared for the tabernacle worship. He doesn't put it on His priests or His people, but the bride pours it out on Him.

"While the king is at his table, my spikenard sends forth its fragrance" foretells an event that happened a few days before Jesus went to Golgotha. The story is found in John 12 and also in Mark 14.

Jesus was in Bethany, which was the city of His friends Mary, Martha, and their brother Lazarus, whom He had raised from the dead. They were making a dinner for Him there with His disciples. Jesus sat at the table.

I'm sure Jesus understood the significance of the time since it was only a few days before Passover and the lamb was being prepared for the sacrifice. I'm not sure Mary understood what was coming, but her sensitivity to the Lord, born of her love for Him, prompted her to offer to Him the most valuable thing she possessed. She broke her bottle of spikenard and poured it out upon His head and feet. She lavished every drop upon Him so the Scripture says, "And the house was filled with the fragrance of the oil" (John 12:3b, NKJV).

Then, in a further display of her devotion, she wiped His feet with her hair. You must understand in her culture a woman's hair was her glory, and to even wash someone's feet was the job of a very lowly servant. Mary poured out on Jesus all she had of love and devotion in absolute humility. She gave it freely, utterly. Mary's love strengthened and encouraged Jesus, helping Him to face the hours soon to come.

When Judas complained about her gift as a waste, saying the perfume should have been sold and the money given to the poor, Jesus replied that she had anointed Him in preparation for the day of His burial. The benefit to Him benefitted multitudes through Him.

Religious duty may encourage us to misdirect the use of our time and resources, but I believe if we intentionally pour out our love and devotion on Jesus with a desire to minister to His heart, all of the needs within our scope of influence will be met as well.

The bride has something she alone can give to the King: her heart poured out in love and devotion. More precious and beautiful than an alabaster flask filled with the rarest perfume, the love of His bride is the treasure most desired by our Lord. At His table, the King enjoys refreshment and fellowship: communion – the joining of hearts. When we meet Him there, we have the opportunity to give to Him the one thing He cannot get for Himself. Every man and woman, boy and girl, has within them the ability to give to the Lord this precious oil.

Much of what we understand about our relationship with Jesus involves what He gives to us, what He does for us. Here is the one thing we can give to Him. It belongs to us to minister to His heart, to pour out on Him all that is within us of devotion, affection, and love. With all my heart, I pray that the fragrance of pure love poured out would once again fill all the house.

COMFORTED

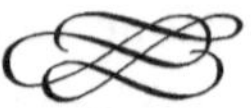

"A bundle of myrrh is my beloved to me,
that lies all night between my breasts" (Song 1:13).

This is the first time the bride speaks of her bridegroom as her beloved. Until this moment she has referred to him as the king. What he has said and done for her has begun to work a change in her heart. She is learning to allow his love to find its way past the barriers of shame, humiliation, and self-preservation that have kept her heart separated from his.

She says he is like a bundle of myrrh that lies all night between her breasts. "A bundle of myrrh" in this instance refers to a healing aromatic. In biblical language "the night" does not speak merely of the hours between sunset and dawn, but allegorically of a time of emotional or spiritual darkness or distress. "Between her breasts" speaks to me of something near to her heart or touching her heart.

I believe what the bride is describing in this passage is her developing trust toward her bridegroom. He is healing the dark places in her heart. She has begun to liken his presence with her to the scent of a soothing and calming aromatic permeating her senses in situations which in the past would have made her feel fearful and alone.

In my own life when depression and anxiety brought about by illness blanketed me like a shroud of darkness until it was a labor to breathe, the only true relief I found was in the comfort of the presence of the Lord. When fear plunged me into a valley filled with shadows, I turned toward Him and saw His face before me. Suddenly, the shadows were not shadows. Jesus filled my valley with His light. In truth I was able to say, "I will fear no evil; for You *are* with me" (Psalm 23:4b, NIV).

I faced the scariest time I had ever known comforted by the vision of His beloved face before me. Jesus was with me through my darkest night. The comfort of His presence filled my senses. His face displaced the buzzing fears that robbed my rest and dismantled my peace.

So, I also pray for you, my friend, that in your darkest hour, as you turn your face toward Him, as you make it an act of your will to give Him your trust and lift up your eyes to see His face, I pray His comfort, even His stillness, will be yours. In the valley of shadows, may His presence fill your darkness with His light.

FORGIVEN

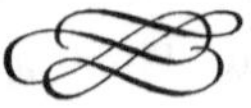

"My beloved is to me a cluster of henna
blooms in the vineyards of En Gedi" (Song 1:14).

King Saul had become a madman and was hunting David to kill him. Saul was tormented by the knowledge that the Lord had left him, and David was to become king in his place.

One day while living as a fugitive, David was hiding in a cave near En Gedi with his men, and Saul came into the cave to relieve himself. While Saul was occupied in this way, David's men encouraged him to see it as an opportunity from God to kill him. David refused to do violence to the king, but he did creep up next to Saul and cut a corner from his robe.

Immediately troubled in his heart over what he had done, David followed Saul out of the cave and called to him, explaining his offense. David then told Saul he intended no harm toward him. Saul answered, ". . . You are more righteous than I; for you have rewarded me with good, whereas I have rewarded you with evil" (1 Samuel 24:17, NKJV). So En Gedi became known as the place where David showed Saul mercy.

Henna (also translated as "camphire") is a fragrant white blossom that, when crushed, produces a reddish dye. It was used in the biblical world as a cosmetic to dye hair, fingernails, and even skin. The word itself comes from the Hebrew word "kopher," which means to cover or coat. It also has the meaning of a redemption price or ransom. The root of "kopher" is "kaphar," which means to placate or cancel, to make atonement, to cleanse, forgive, pardon, purge, or reconcile.

When the bride says, "My beloved is to me a cluster of henna blooms in the vineyards of En Gedi," she is describing his covering presence that pardons and cleanses, reconciling her to fellowship with him where there is nothing between them to cause distance or distress. He rewards her with good when she doesn't deserve it. She feels his embrace when she knows she has done wrong. His kindness surrounds her, giving her hope and the courage she needs to let go of the things which would hinder their fellowship. The more she knows him, the more she trusts him. Her developing trust is drawing her more deeply into his love.

I remember the day the Lord clearly spoke to my heart and said, "Christy, the devil doesn't play fair. He wants to make you too ashamed to come to me when you have messed up, so he can keep you separated from me. Don't let him. Nothing hurts me like separation. I can deal much better with your sin than with your drawing back in shame."

One of the hardest things for us to overcome in our journey deeper into the heart of God is our shame. We may have allowed ourselves to accept forgiveness for the bad things we have done in our pasts; but for some reason, we expect that once we have received forgiveness for our sins, we should be able to "take it from there." In appreciation for all He has done for us, we think we will suddenly stop sinning and will offer to Him our goodness, or our purity, or our faithfulness.

Sadly, when we discover our inability to produce goodness, we often find ourselves mired in clinging, suffocating shame.

I have been around this bush many times. I repent with tears, find comfort in His love, set my heart to goodness, then stumble, fail, flog myself, and distance myself from the Lord until I miss Him so much, I cry out to Him and once again find myself surrounded in His love and forgiveness. Yet in the restoration to fellowship with Him, I have often maintained a hold on shame. It is just so difficult to accept the truth that I am unable to produce goodness.

I have discovered it is pride that urges me to insist on maintaining a hold on my personal goodness. Perhaps we share this failing. Do you find when you fall short time and again, that you shame yourself? Ah, and then shame creates a distance between your heart and God's? I know. It is a penance – a punishment to ourselves – this separation from His heart. But did you know this distance causes Him pain?

Here is a doorway into the heart of God that releases us from what would separate our hearts from His: "My beloved is to me a cluster of henna blooms in the vineyards of En Gedi." He is more righteous than I, for He rewards me with good when I would reward myself with evil. He covers me in white blossoms that bleed red and serve as my ransom. As I enter this place in Him, I am cleansed. All my wrong-doing has been paid for. All my shame is forgotten.

This is not a place to visit. This is a place to live every day in Him. He becomes to us a covering that ransoms our hearts from sin. As we stay in this place of mercy when shame would taunt us to leave it, we learn that God is not troubled by our sin.

When I talk to God about the sin that troubles me, He never enters the horror, disgust, or appall I feel toward myself. Instead, He gently cleanses me. Then He heals my heart and leads me on with reassuring words and a comforting touch while I am kept in His embrace. He is my hiding place from sin, my henna blossoms in the vineyards of En Gedi.

TRANSFORMATION

"Behold, you are fair, my love! Behold, you are fair!
You have dove's eyes" (Song 1:15).

Suddenly the bridegroom cries out, "Look at you! My beautiful one! Just look at the way you glow! You have the beauty of the Holy one in your eyes."

The Hebrew word for "fair" (yaphah) literally means "to be bright." A radiance has come upon the countenance of the bride. She is being transformed in her bridegroom's presence. What has brought about this change? Simply that the bride has turned her eyes toward her beloved. She has filled her vision with him, and as she keeps her eyes fixed on him, she is being transformed into his likeness.

The Holy Spirit is likened to a dove in several places in Scripture. Dove's eyes speak of the beauty of the Spirit of God shining through a person's soul. But another interesting point is that dove's eyes are fixed in their sockets. They don't shift side to side. In 2 Corinthians 3:18 (NKJV), we are told that as we behold the glory of the Lord, we "are being transformed into the same image from glory to glory, just as by the Spirit of the Lord."

The bride has turned her gaze to her beloved. She has filled her vision with his beauty, and as a result his beauty has begun working within her to transform her into the likeness of himself. The bridegroom is delighted with the light he sees in her. Her loveliness increases with every step she takes toward him, with every place in her heart where she gives him her trust.

"Behold, you are handsome, my beloved! Yes, pleasant!" (Song 1:16).

The bride has been filling her heart with the things her bridegroom has come to mean to her. She is wearing the adornment he provided for her, the silver and the gold. She is learning to make a place in her heart for the hope he holds for her, his expectation for the goodness that he sees regarding her. She remembers when he held her through the night as she wrestled the demons of her past. His kindness and reassurance amazed her when her own lack of goodness left her disillusioned with herself. She is beginning to truly see him and to grasp his commitment to her. So she says, "Behold, you are handsome, my beloved! Yes, pleasant!" Or, in other words, "Look at you, my loved one. You are the radiant one! You are so very beautiful."

COVENANT

"The bride says, 'Our bed is green. The beams of our houses
are cedar, and our rafters of fir'" (Song 1:16-17).

I love the way Scripture explains Scripture. To find the key
that opens the door into this passage, I went to Revelation
4. There John describes seeing "a throne set in heaven . . . and there
was a rainbow around the throne, in appearance like an emerald"
(Revelation 4:2-3, NKJV). The rainbow around the throne looked like
an emerald. In other words, the sign of God's deep commitment to us,
His bow set in the heavens so much in evidence around His throne,
has the glow of a deeply green jewel.

Green is a color we associate with life and growth, with verdant
meadows and budding flowers. It carries with it the expectation of
fruitfulness and sustained life. It is also the color of faithfulness. Evergreen trees keep their color year-round. Green speaks of commitment
and constancy. Like the rainbow around the throne, it illustrates
covenant.

When the bride says, "Our bed is green," she is speaking of both the
level of commitment between them and of the promise of fruitfulness

from their union. Their bed is a place of rest and repose. It is also a place of intimacy. New life is the natural result of their coming together in this way. Creativity flows from intimacy.

In the passages "our bed is green" and "the beams of our houses are cedar, and our rafters of fir," we see the bride taking ownership of the home her bridegroom has given her. She speaks of "our bed" and "our houses," and no longer of "the king's chamber."

Both cedar and fir are evergreen trees. The reference is once again to covenant commitment in their union. Cedar beams and fir rafters are solid and beautiful. Her bridegroom has provided her with a home in which she feels safe and secure. No longer will she dwell in tents, nor be exposed to the whims of nature. She has a secure dwelling place in the heart of the one who loves her. He has brought her to live in a place where his unchangeable commitment surrounds and covers her. She is learning to rest in the heart of her bridegroom.

Jesus said, "Abide in Me" (John 15:4a, NKJV). There is a place in Him for each of us, a place where rest becomes fruitful, and life is born out of our trust. When we discover the unfailing commitment of God toward us and allow ourselves to give Him the right to take care of us, we will be able to say, "Our bed is green, the beams of our houses are cedar, and our rafters overhead are fir."

BLOSSOMING

"I am the rose of Sharon, and the lily of the valleys" (Song 2:1).

These words of the bride have often been misapplied to the bridegroom. But it is, in fact, the bride who likens herself to the wildflowers that bloom in such abundance every spring. That she describes herself as a flower shows she has begun to believe the look of appreciation for her beauty that she sees in her bridegroom's eyes. The flowers she speaks of are beautiful and delicate, but common. They are found in every field. Often overlooked, they are even walked upon. I believe she is saying she may have a certain beauty that has attracted the attention of her bridegroom, but she still sees herself as common, nothing so very unusual or special.

"Like a lily among thorns,
so is my love among the daughters" (Song 2:2).

The bridegroom answers that he has found a beautiful treasure in the midst of a barren wasteland. Thorns are neither fruit nor flower. They do not receive the morning dew, nor turn their faces toward the sun. The flower the bridegroom has found is one whose heart is filled with life and light, one who responds to the light of his countenance and to the freshening dew of his presence. He doesn't say he plucked her from the thorns; merely that the contrast of her response to his love next to the indifference of others is as vivid as a flower in the midst of thorns.

The bride responds, "Like an apple tree among the trees of the woods, so is my beloved among the sons. I sat down in his shade with great delight, and his fruit was sweet to my taste" (Song 2:3).

Consider with me what it would be like to walk in a forest for a long time. As you walk, you become thirsty and eventually hungry, yet there is nothing nearby to offer any sustenance. Then suddenly, unexpectedly, you come upon a tree loaded with apples. What a joy and relief it would be to be refreshed and strengthened by its fruit in the midst of your weary wandering. That is the picture the bride is presenting.

The bride has found in her bridegroom someone who is unlike any other. He does not seek her company for what he can get from her. He seeks her out to give to her, care for her, cover her in his shade. In no other has she found the refreshment and rest that she finds in him. In him she has found a home. In him she has found a love that gives her life.

"He brought me to the banqueting house,
and his banner over me was love" (Song 2:4).

"Banqueting house" (in Hebrew, 'yayin') means "house of wine." Wine is symbolically used in Scripture to speak of the joy and well-being we experience in the presence of the Lord. Paul exhorts the Ephesians, "And do not be drunk with wine . . . but be filled with the Spirit" (Ephesians 5:18, NKJV). The things they were looking for in the wine (the freedom from cares, the relief from pain, the sense of lightheartedness) was theirs to be had in a much better way in the in-filling presence of the Spirit of God.

In this verse the bride is saying, "He has brought me to a place where his presence swallows all of my sadness and cares. He has surrounded me with a sense of well-being and filled me with his joy. He has made a declaration over me that I am his beloved."

There are two words for "banner" in the Old Testament: "Nes" is the military banner the army marched under, while "degel" is the banner that identified the tribes. Hebrew tradition holds that the images on the banners under which the tribes camped in the wilderness were a man, an eagle, an ox, and a lion. In Numbers 2:2 we read about the arrangement of the camps. The Lord's instructions state, "Every one of the children of Israel shall camp by his own standard, beside the emblems of his father's house." These emblems bore the same images as the faces of the four living beings or cherubim described in Ezekiel's vision (Ezekiel 1:10).

We are not told what image was on the banner over the bride, only that the banner (degel) over her was love. But 1 John 3:1-2 (NKJV) says, "Behold what manner of love the Father has bestowed on us, that we should be called children of God! . . . It has not yet been revealed what we shall be, but we know that when He is revealed, we shall be like Him, for we shall see Him as He is."

Degel, the banner under which the bride was found, was the "emblem of her father's house." First John 4:8 states, "God is love." The emblem of our Father's house, the "degel" under which we are identified by our tribe, is love. We are recognized as the beloved of God by the enemies who come against us. We are seen as the heart's delight of the one who has given His love to us as a shield and a shade. He flies His banner above us that all may see we are truly the beloved children of our Father.

HUNGERING

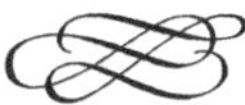

"Sustain me with cakes of raisins,
refresh me with apples,
for I am lovesick" (Song 2:5).

Raisin cakes, or flagons, were a pressed cake of dried grapes or figs. The other reference to them in Scripture was at a time of celebration on the day following the restoration of the Ark of the Covenant to Jerusalem, when David gave to each person a loaf of bread, a piece of meat, and a cake of raisins (2 Samuel 6:19). Raisin cakes were a delicacy, distributed in celebration of the presence of the Lord coming to abide in the midst of His people.

The bride asks for raisin cakes and apples. Raisins are nutritious and sustaining, and apples, juicy and sweet, are a refreshing fruit, but I love the implication that the bride is not actually asking for food for her body.

Earlier she states that her bridegroom is like an apple tree among the trees of the wood. She sat in his shade and his fruit was sweet to her taste. The bride is weak with love. She is overcome by what she is experiencing. For the first time in her life, love has overwhelmed her, and she is robbed of her strength. But instead of sending away the one who has so overwhelmed her, she asks for more.

By asking, "Sustain me with cakes of raisins, refresh me with apples," I believe the bride is saying, "Fill me with the sweetness of your presence. Give me more of yourself. I am filled, but not sated. I am weak with love for you, and only you can answer the yearning you have created within me."

Dear friend, did you know God loves to give Himself to you? Did you know you can never have too much of God? I remember when I began to learn this.

I had received prayer just for a blessing – a gift because it was my birthday. The Holy Spirit began to touch me with His weighty glory until I bowed and finally lay upon the floor. Then I saw the Lord putting jewels inside my being. The jewels were all very large, golf ball-sized, of different cuts and colors. There were diamonds, sapphires, rubies, emeralds, topazes; all colors and types of stones were being poured into my being.

At first, I was delighted, but after a while I thought, "It is too much." So, I said to the Lord, "Stop. It is enough. You are giving me too much!" Then in my spirit I heard Jesus say to me, "Oh no. Let me give you more. I want to give you more."

I will never forget the sound in His voice. He spoke with such joy in the giving, but also there was a catch of yearning there. It delighted Him to give to me, and it would have grieved Him if I had stopped Him before He had done all for me that He wished. So, I lay still and received, and received, and received. He gave to His heart's delight, and I would not tell Him "No." It was a heart exchange. He was loving me by giving me His treasures, and I was loving Him by receiving all He longed to give.

He is more generous than we can comprehend, yet what we taste of Him creates a desire for more. The yearning becomes an insatiable hunger until the words of the bride resonate within us, "I am lovesick," and we find ourselves crying out, "More, Lord! Please give me more of you!" It is His delight to give Himself and His treasures to those He loves.

EMBRACED

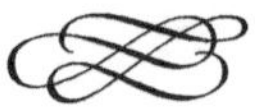

"His left hand is under my head,
and his right hand embraces me" (Song 2:6).

To understand the significance of this verse, we have to look for a moment at two passages in the book of Genesis. The first is found in chapter 41, where the Bible records the names of the sons of Joseph born to him while serving in Pharaoh's house. The first he called Manasseh, which means "forgetful," for he said, "God has made me forget all of my toil and all of my father's house." The second he called Ephraim, which means "fruitfulness," for, Joseph said, "God has caused me to be fruitful in the land of my affliction."

Manasseh represented to Joseph freedom from the pain and sorrow of his past. Ephraim represented the promise and hope of a life rich in fulfillment.

Now look with me in Genesis 48. Joseph has been reunited with his father, Israel, after many years of separation. Throughout those years Joseph had not even the hope of seeing his father alive again. Now

Joseph has brought his two sons to Israel to receive his father's blessing. Traditionally, the firstborn would receive the blessing of the right hand, while the second would be touched by the left hand. Although Joseph presented his sons each on the correct side of his father, Israel crossed his hands and gave the right-hand blessing to the younger. So, it became the blessing passed through the history of the people that "fruitfulness" is associated with the right hand, while "forgetfulness" is tied to the left.

Now look again at this verse from Song: "His left hand (forgetfulness) is under my head, and his right hand (fruitfulness) embraces me."

We are cradled in the arms of our Beloved, as He chases away dark and painful memories, causing us to forget the brokenness of our pasts. In His arms our futures are bright with hope and the promise of fulfillment. Where we were once empty and alone, fruitfulness fills our lives. This is His promise to each of us.

REST

"I charge you, O daughters of Jerusalem,
by the gazelles or by the does of the field,
do not stir up nor awaken love until it pleases" (Song 2:7).

Here the bride is saying to those who are anxious to taste the joys of marriage that love is not something one can force or pursue. Like the gazelles or does of the field that draw near in the stillness, love comes quietly and surrounds us in rest. She seems to be saying that if you would find love, quiet your heart and it will come to you. Truly, this is the way into the peace of God.

It is human nature, I suppose, to frantically pursue that which we lack. I have tried many times to find my way into the rest of God when I was troubled or afraid, finally giving up in exhaustion, then to discover He was holding me all along, and I had only to be still for the sense of His peace and love to fill me.

This was brought home very clearly to me once when I was feeding my infant son who was a very impatient eater. I guided the nipple into his mouth and waited for him to begin to suck. But oblivious to the fact that what he wanted was already his to have, he continued to thrash and flail and cry, convinced I was ignoring his needs. I waited, holding him, trying to quiet him, until he realized everything he needed was already there. Once he stopped crying and began to feed, the Lord spoke to my heart saying I was often like that with Him. All I needed and wanted was already mine. I had only to be still in order to experience it.

Amy Carmichael wrote in her little book, *If*, "Love is pressing 'round us on all sides like air. Cease to resist, and instantly love takes possession."[1]

The question is not whether we are loved. We are! It is not something we have to seek as if it has gone missing. We do not need to stir up love and rouse it to come to us. Instead, we should take a lesson from the does of the field. When we have quieted ourselves, we will be filled with the Love who waits for us to cease our striving, let down our defenses, and believe that what He says of us is true.

When this section ends, the bride is lying in the arms of her beloved, deeply satisfied in his love. His love for her has begun to overcome her sense of shame over her past failings and lack of goodness. She has begun to receive his assessment of her value. She is basking in the love that holds her close in the darkness and causes her to forget the reasons she cried.

She is experiencing a sense of well-being in this love that has made a place for her that is hers alone, a place so suited to her in every way that she is cradled in a cocoon of peace. She has begun to hold an expectation of good for her life. With her beloved she is looking forward to a life of fruitfulness and fulfillment. She sleeps in the arms of her beloved, sated in the love that has captivated her heart. This is the beginning of intimacy.

PART II

SONG OF SOLOMON 2:8 – 3:5, NKJV

The voice of my beloved!
Behold, he comes
Leaping upon the mountains,
Skipping upon the hills.
My beloved is like a gazelle or a young stag.
Behold, he stands behind our wall;
He is looking through the windows,
Gazing through the lattice.
My beloved spoke, and said to me:
"Rise up, my love, my fair one,
And come away.
For lo, the winter is past,
The rain is over and gone.
The flowers appear on the earth;
The time of singing has come,
And the voice of the turtledove
Is heard in our land.
The fig tree puts forth her green figs,

And the vines with the tender grapes
Give a good smell.
Rise up, my love, my fair one,
And come away!
O my dove, in the clefts of the rock,
In the secret places of the cliff,
Let me see your face,
Let me hear your voice;
For your voice is sweet,
And your face is lovely.
Catch us the foxes,
The little foxes that spoil the vines,
For our vines have tender grapes."

My beloved is mine, and I am his.
He feeds his flock among the lilies.
Until the day breaks
And the shadows flee away,
Turn, my beloved,
And be like a gazelle
Or a young stag
Upon the mountains of Bether.
By night on my bed I sought the one I love;
I sought him, but I did not find him.
'I will rise now,' I said,
'And go about the city;
In the streets and in the squares
I will seek the one I love.'
I sought him but I did not find him.
The watchmen who go about the city found me;
I said, 'Have you seen the one I love?'
Scarcely had I passed by them,
When I found the one I love.
I held him and would not let him go,
Until I had brought him to the house of my mother,

And into the chamber of her who conceived me.

I charge you, O daughters of Jerusalem,
By the gazelles or by the does of the field,
Do not stir up nor awaken love
Until it pleases.

LITTLE FOXES

$\mathcal{M}$any years ago, when our children were small, my family spent a week vacationing at my parents' cabin in the mountains of eastern Oregon. One afternoon we decided to take a walk. My husband had been on one of the logging roads behind the cabin on a motorcycle and thought it would be a fun road to hike. Not realizing how much farther the distance would seem for small people walking than it had been on a bike, we set out.

Six-year-old Ben and five-year-old Andy did well scampering over logs, hunting huckleberries, and hiking up hills and through marshes, but for three-year-old Tucker's short little legs, the journey became very long. Finally, after bravely struggling along for what must have seemed like hours with no cabin in sight, Tucker wearily said to his dad, "Daddy, this road is too big for me." Instantly, Tucker found himself atop his father's shoulders. Carried along in long, sure strides, the rest of the journey became a game. The struggle was over. Tucker was at rest and looked down at the ground we were covering with triumphant glee.

I have often thought of that day in the years that followed. Many times, overwhelmed with the journey of my life, I borrowed Tucker's words to cry out to my Father, "Daddy, this road is too big for me." It has taken me a long time to realize that my Father never intended that I walk my road in my strength alone. It has always been His intention to take me on my journey.

Every day He invites me to join Him in the things He is doing. In accepting His invitation I can only depend upon Him for the strength and grace needed to walk there. Where He is going is beyond my ability to accompany Him. He must take me there. This is something the bride will soon discover.

In the opening verses of this section of the Song, the bride is reveling in the memory of the night in her lover's arms. She is lying in her bed when she hears his voice outside. "The voice of my beloved! Behold he comes leaping upon the mountains, skipping upon the hills. My beloved is like a gazelle or a young stag" (Song 2:8-9). She looks and sees him coming down from the heights. He is beautiful to her. She watches him with pleasure, enjoying his strength and grace.

"He is looking through the windows, gazing through the lattice" (Song 2:9). He has risen from their bed and gone out in the early morning hours. But he returns for her and invites her to join him. He doesn't come back to their chamber but stands outside waiting for her to come out to him.

He speaks and says, "Rise up, my love, my fair one, and come away. For lo, the winter is past, the rain is over and gone. The flowers appear on the earth; the time of singing has come, and the voice of the turtledove is heard in our land. The fig tree puts forth her green figs, and the vines with the tender grapes give a good smell. Rise up, my love, my fair one, and come away!" (Song 2:10-13).

He tells her there is great beauty beyond their door, life to experience. There is much he wants to show her, to share with her. It is springtime. New life is budding forth. The dormancy of winter is past. The voice of the turtle dove speaks of the Spirit of God giving voice to His creative word. There is hope and the promise of a future filled with fruitfulness before her, and he says to her, "Come with me."

But she neither answers him, nor moves to go to him. So, he continues to entreat her by saying, "O my dove, in the clefts of the rock, in the secret places of the cliff, let me see your face, let me hear your voice; for your voice is sweet, and your face is lovely" (Song 2:14).

He is saying, "My darling, come with me to the heights, and I want to share my secrets with you. I want you with me. You are the one who delights my heart. I want to share my life with you." In calling the bride His dove, the Lord is saying she has the Holy Spirit within her. There is nothing limiting her from going with Him, because the Holy Spirit is able to take her where He is going.

He wants her to come with Him to the clefts of the rock. Jesus is inviting, even entreating, His bride to take the place that will help her the most. To go to the cleft of the rock and the secret place in the heights is to be found in Jesus. He never intended His bride to arrive in these places without Him. He is not asking her to meet Him there. He is asking if she will accompany Him there.

Still, the bride makes no move to go with him, nor answers him at all. So, he says, "Catch us the foxes, the little foxes that spoil the vines, for our vines have tender grapes" (Song 2:15). He likens the thoughts that are holding her back from joining him to the foxes that come and eat the grapes while they are still in their formative stages. These thieves, though small, are very effective at spoiling the fruitfulness of a crop. There is something in the bride that is causing her to hesitate, and the bridegroom sees it as robbery.

At last the bride speaks, but it is not to answer his invitation. Instead, she maintains her position in a truth she had discovered in the days before: "My beloved is mine, and I am his. He feeds his flock among the lilies" (Song 2:16).

She has a claim upon him and a certain confidence in the place she holds in his heart. She believes she knows where he will be and that she will be able to find him there when she chooses to leave their chamber. So she sends him away with the words, "Until the day breaks and the shadows flee away, turn, my beloved, and be like a gazelle or a young stag upon the mountains of Bether" (Song 2:17).

I don't think the bride is trying to break fellowship with him. She doesn't see how she can go with him. He is obviously suited to traveling on the heights that he wants so much to share with her, but she knows herself. She knows what her limitations are, and not seeing how she can go with him, she sends him away.

"Bether" in Hebrew means cleavage, or separation. She sees the mountains as something that divides them. He is going there, and she must stay behind. But she is not too troubled by this because she expects to continue to see him in the places she has been accustomed to finding him.

It is not until days and nights have passed without him appearing that she becomes aware something has changed in their relationship. She discovers that his call to join him beyond their walls is not optional. She has been expecting him to come to her in the familiar places, but he has not come. Now although she still cannot see how she is to do what he is asking, she goes out to seek him and find what she must do to have him in her life again.

The bride says, "By night on my bed I sought the one I love; I sought him, but I did not find him. I said, 'I will rise now and go about the city; in the streets and in the squares I will seek the one I love.' I sought him, but I did not find him. The watchmen who go about the city found me; I asked them, 'Have you seen the one I love?' Scarcely had I passed by them, when I found the one I love" (Song 3:1-3).

She sought him in the city streets and squares but did not find him. Finally, she asked the men who keep watch over the city if they had seen the one she loves. Immediately after speaking to them, she finds him. I think he was always near, waiting for her to come to him. I believe he was nearby as she wandered the streets and squares in her silent search. When she acknowledged she was searching for her bridegroom, he stepped out of the shadows and showed himself to her.

"I held him and would not let him go, until I had brought him to the house of my mother, and into the chamber of her who conceived me" (Song 3:4). When at last she finds him, she clings to him and takes him to her home.

HIS VOICE

"The voice of my beloved . . ." (Song 2:8).

One night on a stormy sea, twelve men rowed against the wind. They had rowed all night and made little progress. Though exhausted, they continued toiling with the oars throughout the night, fighting the waves. In the early hours, shortly before dawn, one of the men looked out through the spray and saw what appeared to be an apparition walking toward them on the surface of the sea. In disbelief he pointed and called to the others to look. They saw it too. Convinced they were seeing a ghost, they cried out in fear. But Jesus called out to them, "Have courage. It is I; do not be afraid." Then Peter answered, "Lord, if it is you, command me to come to you on the water." Jesus said, "Come." So, Peter stepped out of the boat and walked toward Jesus on the water (Matthew 14:22-33, *paraphrased*).

When I was a very young Christian, there was a teaching prevalent in the church that we should "step out in faith" like Peter had. We were taught that once we had decided the direction in which we thought

God wanted us to go, then we should set things in motion for it to happen and trust Him to work miracles on our behalf. It sounded pretty good in theory; but I saw a lot of casualties of that teaching, and my own faith suffered some pretty extreme blows before I discovered the truth about that night upon the Sea of Galilee.

What we had forgotten to take into account was the pivotal point of the narrative. Before Peter stepped out of the boat, he asked Jesus to tell him to come to Him, and Jesus said, "Come." It is my belief Peter may have walked on water in the physical sense, but what he stepped out on was the word of the Lord. It was the word Jesus spoke that gave him the courage to get out of the boat, and it was His word that supported him in the waves.

I no longer believe there is such a thing as "blind faith," or that "stepping out in faith" involves determining what we want God to do and then creating a situation in which we force Him to come through. But I very much believe it is my privilege and joy to walk in the places where Jesus' words precede me. Now when I am faced with any situation that requires divine intervention, I don't tell God what I want Him to do. I have learned to first ask what He wants to do, wait to hear His word, and then walk there. Like Peter, I can have confidence to stand in an impossible place by the word of the Lord.

But what has all this to do with the bride? I believe this is the lesson she must learn in the second part of this journey: to hear His word and believe it. When we believe in something, we put our weight upon it. We allow it to support us and hold us up. We can even walk upon it when there seems to be nothing else beneath our feet.

When we believe the spoken (rhema) word, we are changed by it. (Rhema is Greek for the word given to us by the Holy Spirit in a specific moment and situation). By the spoken word of God, Gideon was taken from hiding in the winepress to leading an army of three hundred men into battle against a multitude. It was the word of God that brought Moses back to Pharaoh's court after forty years of hiding on the back side of the desert. It was the specific spoken word of God that gave Abram (which means "exalted father") the courage to change his name to Abraham ("father of a multitude") and to wait for twenty-five years from the time he was first given the promise for Sarah to have their son. He had no evidence of his declaration that he was the patriarch of a people other than the promise God had spoken.

The bride hears the voice of her beloved. His invitation to join him couldn't be clearer. She has actually heard many words spoken by her beloved that would help her to follow him now, but something is hindering her. He invites but does not insist. The choice to go with him must be hers. The choice to move into deeper intimacy always belongs to the bride. Our Bridegroom has called us each to a place in Him of dizzying heights, but the choice remains with us whether we will trust Him to take us there.

Sadly, the bride stays behind her wall and listens to her beloved's words, never allowing them to *kiss* her so his courage may come into her. She listens as he tells her about the springtime outside, the wonders which await her. It sounds lovely, but she has forgotten that his name is ointment poured forth, supplying her every need. She still believes she is small and dark and common. She forgot to look and see the promise she was in his eyes. She has forgotten she is gowned and jeweled, draped in gold and silver, as a fitting companion – in every way suitable to stand by his side.

She has been comfortable and happy with him in the privacy of their chamber. Now she sees his strength and grace as he moves upon the mountains. He leaps with ease from one craggy height to another, but she knows she has never been strong. She cannot follow him there.

These are the little foxes nibbling away at the tender plants. These are the voices in her head attempting to destroy her budding faith before it has a chance to flower. If successful, these little foxes will keep her back from becoming all that her bridegroom has intended. The bridegroom even entreats her to come with him to the secret place; he says it is her voice he longs to hear there, and her face he longs to see.

My own heart turns over with longing at these words. Many times I have neglected the desire of my Love to see me in the secret place and to hear my voice there. Many times I have turned to this passage and discovered it has been too long since I journeyed there with Him. Life is full of distractions which keep me from the secret place. I have even forgotten sometimes that life with Him is only found in the cleft of the Rock.

In Exodus 33, God has a conversation with Moses about the things He desires Israel to understand and to do. At the end of this dialogue, Moses asks God, "Please, show me your glory." God answers that He will make all of His goodness pass before Moses and He will proclaim His name. Then in verse 22, God says, ". . . I will put you in the cleft of the rock, and will cover you with My hand while I pass by" (NKJV).

It was God who put Moses in the cleft of the rock. It is God who covers each of us with His hand and draws us into the secret place with Him. But we must respond when He calls. We have to say "yes" to His expressed longing.

This place in God is not attained through our ability. It is found when we follow His voice and give our trust to Him. We can go to Him outside our walls, outside our usual limits. We can follow Him on to the heights because His voice has preceded us there. He said, "Come." Now the heights belong to us. We can step into any place where we have heard His voice say, "Come!"

Each of us discovers this in our own way. For many of us, it is a painful lesson learned through a time of separation from the presence of the Lord. The bride sent her bridegroom away because she didn't believe she could follow him. She had expected to continue to enjoy his fellowship in the places she had always found him to be, but he was not there when she went to their usual trysting place. His scent was no longer on her pillow. His whispers were no longer in her ear. She missed him and cried out for him to come back to her, but only the silence answered.

I have experienced this pain, as I expect most of my readers have. It is a time of bewilderment for us. We are being asked to do something we don't believe we can do, and we find ourselves adrift until we set ourselves to begin. Usually, it is a measure of the strength of our wills that determines how long we stay in this place. God is patient and waits for us to trust Him, and as soon as we do, our faith finds a foothold that we had no idea was there. Then we discover we are able to go where we had thought we could not.

VENTURE FORTH

"I will rise now . . . I will seek the one I love," the bride says.
"I sought him, but I did not find him. The watchmen who go about the
city found me; I said, 'Have you seen the one I love?' Scarcely had
I passed by them, when I found the one I love" (Song 3:2-4).

She wanders about looking for her love, but it is not until she asks the men who keep watch in the city that she finds him. Confessing her need caused her bridegroom to appear.

I believe Jesus waits for us to move toward that to which He calls us, and as soon as we begin, He is there to help us. Like the father daily watching the horizon for the return of his prodigal son and running to meet him with a robe and a ring, our Father waits for us to turn toward Him and races to greet us at the first sound of our voice.

The battle with our wills is ours to win, but once we have set our hearts to follow Him, He is with us all of the way. This battle to bring our hearts into agreement with God is something Jesus understands. Remember Gethsemane? He offers His help to us even in this.

"When I found the one I love I held him and would not let him go, until I had brought him to the house of my mother, and into the chamber of her who conceived me" (Song 3:4). The bride found her love and took him home with her, which seems to be only logical, but there is something in the wording of this passage that caught my eye. Why did she take him to her mother's house and to the chamber where she was conceived? Why didn't they return to their own marriage bed, to the home they shared together?

I believe in bringing her bridegroom to this place the bride is giving him access to the foundations of her life. She is giving him the keys to her heart and is allowing all she was before he was her husband to be affected by his presence in her life.

The hidden things of our pasts must be given to the one who loves us if we are ever to be free to go with Him where He leads. It was the person she was before she was his that prevented the bride from going with her bridegroom to the mountains. By bringing him to the place where she was conceived, she was giving him access to her history.

When Jesus enters our histories, we are never the same again. Inviting His presence into childhood memories floods our darkness with His light. When we give Him access to the hidden places of our hearts, He reaches in and transforms our perceptions of what was true in those situations, as well as our perceptions of who we are. By changing the understanding of our history, He sets us free from the limitations that dictate the borders of our lives.

This section closes with the same words we find in the first section. The bride says, "I charge you, O daughters of Jerusalem, by the gazelles or by the does of the field, do not stir up nor awaken love until it pleases" (Song 3:5). But this time, though the words are the same, the bride means something different by them. "Do not stir up nor awaken love until it pleases" can also imply this is not a love to be trifled with. She seems to be saying, "Be very sure this is what you want, for this love will require all you have to give."

Once again, the bride rests in the arms of her beloved, but it is not the same as before. She has gained a new place in her journey. She may have missed traveling to the heights, but she has taken important steps into intimacy. She has wrestled with and overcome the fears her soul once held before her, which caused her to lose fellowship with her beloved. She has flung wide the door of a history which once held her hostage. She has invited the one who makes all things new into the hidden places of her past, and she has begun to enter into a liberty she had never imagined was possible.

PART III

SONG OF SOLOMON 3:6 – 5:1, NKJV

Who is this coming out of the wilderness
Like pillars of smoke,
Perfumed with myrrh and frankincense,
With all the merchant's fragrant powders?
Behold, it is Solomon's couch,
With sixty valiant men around it, of the valiant of Israel.
They all hold swords, being expert in war.
Every man has his sword on his thigh
Because of fear in the night.
Of the wood of Lebanon Solomon the King
Made himself a palanquin:
He made its pillars of silver,
Its support of gold,
Its seat of purple,
Its interior paved with love
By the daughters of Jerusalem.
Go forth, O daughters of Zion,
And see King Solomon with the crown
With which his mother crowned him

On the day of his wedding,
The day of the gladness of his heart.

Behold, you are fair, my love!
Behold, you are fair!
You have dove's eyes behind your veil.
Your hair is like a flock of goats,
Going down from Mount Gilead.
Your teeth are like a flock of shorn sheep

Which have come up from the washing,
Every one of which bears twins,
And none is barren among them.
Your lips are like a strand of scarlet,
And your mouth is lovely.
Your temples behind your veil
Are like a piece of pomegranate.
Your neck is like the tower of David,
Built for an armory,
On which hang a thousand bucklers,
All shields of mighty men.
Your two breasts are like two fawns,
Twins of a gazelle,
Which feed among the lilies.

Until the day breaks
And the shadows flee away,
I will go my way to the mountain of myrrh
And to the hill of frankincense.

You are all fair, my love,
And there is no spot in you.
Come with me from Lebanon, my spouse,
With me from Lebanon.
Look from the top of Amana,

From the top of Senir and Hermon,
From the lions' dens,
From the mountains of the leopards.
You have ravished my heart,
My sister, my spouse;
You have ravished my heart
With one look of your eyes,
With one link of your necklace.

How fair is your love,
My sister, my spouse!
How much better than wine is your love,
And the scent of your perfumes than all spices!
Your lips, O my spouse,
Drip as the honeycomb;
Honey and milk are under your tongue;
And the fragrance of your garments
Is like the fragrance of Lebanon.
A garden enclosed
Is my sister, my spouse,
A spring shut up,
A fountain sealed.
Your plants are an orchard of pomegranates
With pleasant fruits,
Fragrant henna with spikenard,
Spikenard and saffron,
Calamus and cinnamon,
With all trees of frankincense,
Myrrh and aloes,
With all the chief spices –
A fountain of gardens,
A well of living waters,
And streams from Lebanon.

Awake, O north wind,

And come, O south!
Blow upon my garden,
That its spices may flow out.
Let my beloved come to his garden
And eat its pleasant fruits.

I have come to my garden, my sister, my spouse;
I have gathered my myrrh with my spice;
I have eaten my honeycomb with my honey;
I have drunk my wine with my milk.

Eat, O friends!
Drink, yes, drink deeply,
O beloved ones!

THE WILDERNESS

"Who is this coming out of the wilderness like pillars of smoke, perfumed with myrrh and frankincense, with all the merchant's fragrant powders? Behold, it is Solomon's couch, with sixty valiant men around it, of the valiant of Israel. They all hold swords, being expert in war. Every man has his sword on his thigh because of fear in the night" (Song 3:6-8).

At the close of the last section, we saw the bride giving the bridegroom access to the hidden things of her past. This was an act of great vulnerability, the evidence of a deep trust toward her beloved. Or, perhaps, more accurately, the longing for her bridegroom overcame the fear of her past. She was forced to make the choice between giving him her heart and losing his nearness. For one in-love, there is no question in this choice; only in finding the courage to carry it out.

The bride's choice to become vulnerable to her bridegroom has set the stage for what we see happening now. At the opening of this scene, they are coming up out of the wilderness. What has happened between the night in her mother's room and this very public processional complete with military escort? I will attempt to fill in the blanks.

"Behold, I will allure her, will bring her into the wilderness,
and speak comfort to her" (Hosea 2:14, NKJV).

The wilderness has ever been the place God meets with His beloved to unveil His heart. Whenever God has secrets to impart, He draws His loved one away to a lonely place. The Hebrew word for wilderness is "Midbar." It has the meaning of an uninhabited place without reference to the availability or lack of vegetation, water, or animal life. It can also be interpreted as "pasture" – a place for grazing flocks or cattle.

It was in the wilderness God spoke to Moses, commissioning him to return with His people to that lonely place to worship Him. In the wilderness God made Himself known to His people – revealing His power to deliver, His ability to provide, and His desire to care for all their needs. God wanted His people to come apart from the clamoring influences on their lives to worship.

The Greek word for worship is "proskuneo," which means, "to turn toward and kiss." It speaks of giving honor, of showing deference and paying homage to one worthy of reverence. But I believe it is God's desire that His people take a step nearer to Him in worship. We may come before Him bowing and giving Him honor, but He wants to embrace us in His love. The night the bride gave her bridegroom the keys to her past was the night she truly turned toward him and kissed him.

There is nothing more beautiful to our God than a heart turned toward Him in trust. Flinging aside all self-protection and giving ourselves over to the care of the one who loves us is the most difficult and amazing thing we will ever experience. Difficult because to get to that point we have to face our deepest fears and decide in the face of them that He is worthy to be entrusted with their keeping; and amazing, because the response from our God is so immediate and complete, we find ourselves carried away to a secret place in Him. There He peels away the layers over our hearts and teaches us how we may trust Him with those most tender and hidden aspects of our beings.

To be drawn away to a lonely place with God is one of the sweetest and most satisfying experiences in the life of one who loves Him. Jesus frequently went apart to a lonely place with His Father when He was troubled, or in need of His Father's touch. When we draw apart with Him regularly, it becomes the best part of our day. It's a time we learn to look forward to with longing and that we leave reluctantly to take up the duties of the day.

God also arranges wilderness seasons for His loved ones. What we gain in them has much to do with our acceptance of the isolation and our choice to turn toward Him in that place. While we are in the wilderness, there may be little interaction with people to draw on the fullness of our relationship with God. Often, a wilderness season includes a time when God seems far away. We don't hear Him like we once did. We don't feel His presence like we had. The drawing back of His presence makes us wonder if we have done something to lose what was so precious to us. We search our hearts and look for the error asking, "Did I offend you, Lord? Did I displease you in any way?" We look for a return to the former feeling of closeness to the Lord, but God is taking us on. There is no going back. He is making an opportunity for us to know Him in a new way.

I have experienced extended wilderness seasons, admittedly not always with complacence. Sometimes in these seasons I have felt very definitely on the shelf – quite forgotten – but the truth is Jesus has never forgotten me. The wilderness is often not a place that is satisfying to our souls, but it is always enriching to our spirits. I believe the

Lord gives us wilderness seasons to deepen what He wants us to have in Him.

In the wilderness, Jesus takes us from one level of knowing Him to another. There is no other place for this. The things we gain in the secret place with Jesus become the colors of His light we display to the world. Nothing is more beautiful than the light that shines from a life who worships in the wilderness, except the Source of that light Himself.

ROYAL PROCESSION

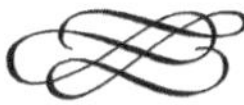

This section opens with the daughters of Jerusalem saying, "Who is this coming out of the wilderness like pillars of smoke, perfumed with myrrh and frankincense, with all the merchant's fragrant powders?" (Song 3:6).

"Pillars of smoke" beautifully references the cloud of God's presence that was visible to all of Israel for the forty years they were in the wilderness. The cloud of His presence never left them. It was a constant reminder to friend and foe that the God of Israel was with them to fight for them and to provide for all their needs.

The bridegroom is perfumed with myrrh and frankincense and with all the merchant's fragrant powders. The merchant's fragrant powders are the valuable spices used for trade. Myrrh, frankincense, and spices were also used in the tabernacle worship – in the anointing oil, in incense, and as offerings to the Lord. That they say he is fragrant with these things declares he is surrounded in the love and worship of his beloved.

The daughters of Jerusalem start this description by asking, "Who is this?" I believe this is a rhetorical question. They see the bride now returning from the wilderness with her bridegroom in royal splendor. The bride has given herself to her bridegroom in an act of deep vulnerability. In response, he took her away to the secret place with him and gave his heart to her in equal measure. Now they are returning from their time of shared intimacy in a royal procession.

The bride returns with a new understanding of her beloved. She acknowledges his faithfulness and his constancy revealed in the pillars of smoke. She recognizes his beauty and worships him as shown by the fragrance that surrounds him. But there is something else she sees now, and I believe it is for the first time. It is a revelation; an unveiling of truth that belongs to her because she has chosen to trust him. This vision of him, the revealing of this facet of his person, will take her on in the way she has chosen to go. She will now know him in this way forever and will build upon this understanding of his character with certainty in her future.

> "Behold, it is Solomon's couch, with sixty valiant men around
> it, of the valiant of Israel. They all hold swords, being
> expert in war. Every man has his sword on his thigh
> because of fear in the night" (Song 3:7-8).

Here, for the first time, the bride sees the Warrior King. Up until now the bride has seen her bridegroom as the Splendid Sovereign, the Nurturing Shepherd, the Loving Husband, but although seeing him in these ways was comforting to her in the moment, they did not sufficiently address the "fear in the night."

God has many names we have learned to love and to rely upon. He is our Healer, our Shepherd, and our Provider. There is, however, one covenant name God calls Himself in reference to His people more often than any other; but it is a name I have rarely heard anyone call upon. He is for us the Lord of Hosts.

Isaiah 54:4-5 (NKJV) entreats us with these words, "Do not fear, for you will not be ashamed; Neither be disgraced, for you will not be put to shame; For you will forget the shame of your youth, And will not remember the reproach of your widowhood anymore. For your Maker *is* your husband, the LORD of hosts *is* His name; And your Redeemer is the Holy One of Israel; He is called the God of the whole earth."

It is the Lord of Hosts the bride now sees coming up with her from the wilderness. He is flanked by sixty mighty warriors, armed and dangerous, who are prepared to fight the "fear in the night."

Six is a number that speaks of the strength of man. Ten refers to what is legal before God, His law and righteousness. Again, we see six times ten. There are sixty mighty warriors; the strength of man moving in the righteous power of God. I believe they are a picture of Jesus, the Son of Man.

They are all expert in war, with their swords on their thighs. Thighs are a reference to strength and the sword is a deadly weapon used both defensively to protect and offensively to overcome the enemy. This awesome show of strength is an illustration of the power of the Lord of Hosts to overcome any threat to the bride. I believe it is God's desire that His people see Him as the Lord of Hosts whenever we are threatened by that which lives in and draws its strength from darkness - the fear in the night.

But while some will see the Lord of Hosts, the rest will only see the reason to fear.

When the children of Israel came out of Egypt, their deliverance came by miraculous signs and the mighty intervention of God. The waters of the Red Sea stood on either side of them as they passed safely through; then they watched as Pharaoh's army gave chase and drowned when the waters came back upon them. They trembled at the base of the mountain filled with thunder and earthquakes and fire as God met with Moses and gave him instructions concerning them. Over and over, God provided for them and kept them safe as they worshiped at His mountain and as they traveled to the land that had been promised to their father, Abraham.

When they arrived at the border, Moses sent twelve men to spy out the land. Ten came back with the report that the land was populated with giants and the land itself devoured its inhabitants. But two, Caleb and Joshua, said the land was exceedingly good, and "if the Lord delights in us then He will bring us into this land and give it to us." Then they said, "Only do not rebel against the LORD, nor fear the people of the land, for they *are* our bread; their protection has departed from them, and the LORD is with us. Do not fear them" (Numbers 14:8-9, NKJV, *paraphrased*).

What was in the hearts of Joshua and Caleb that gave them such a view of the land? What was the difference between them and the ten? I believe the difference was that Joshua and Caleb had not merely endured the exodus and the trembling at the base of the mountain. I believe they had turned their eyes toward the one who was making Himself known to His people in the wilderness. They had filled their vision with Him so much that when they looked at the giants in the land compared to God, they saw them as no threat at all.

The bride, too, has done what Caleb and Joshua did. She has filled her vision with the one who made himself known to her in the wilderness. She has entrusted her heart to him; and in that place of deep devotion, she has discovered he is powerful beyond her ability to imagine.

I have come to recognize that when I feel afraid, I can never bring myself to peace by simply reminding myself of truth. I struggle and struggle and try to change my feelings by sternly taking authority over my thoughts, but it just doesn't work for me. Happily, I have discovered that when I turn my eyes toward Jesus and lay my need to see Him before Him - He comes. I have learned to ask for a new revelation of Him at the times when what I have known beforehand does not answer my need.

The problem is never that He is inadequate to meet my need, but often my knowledge of Him is found to be inadequate to the situation I am facing. The giants loom very large. In my head I know my God is bigger, but until I see His strength summoned on my behalf, until I hear the reminder of His intention to bring everything right, I find I am subject to fear.

The first step toward this revelation is mine to take. I begin by declaring, "God is Good. He is my God, and I will have no other." I choose to give fear to God alone. He is all powerful and no one can stand against Him. This is my confession and I take it to the bank. There I draw upon the truth of who He is and wait until He speaks concerning the giants I am facing.

He has never turned me away or refused to give me the help I need. Instead, He always leads me into His peace and offers me the assurance of His love and interest.

Our peace causes terror in the heart of our enemy, for he sees in our peace the promise of his destruction at the hands of the one who has given us peace (Philippians 1:28).

Behold our king, mighty in strength, surrounding His royal palanquin. He is an expert in war. His sword is on His thigh because of fear in the night.

THE PALANQUIN

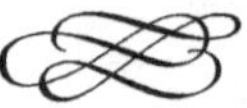

"Of the wood of Lebanon Solomon the King made himself a
palanquin: He made its pillars of silver, its support of gold, its seat of
purple, its interior paved with love by the daughters of Jerusalem. Go
forth, O daughters of Zion, and see King Solomon with the crown
with which his mother crowned him on the day of his wedding,
the day of the gladness of his heart" (Song 3:9-11).

"Of the wood of Lebanon Solomon the King made himself a
palanquin." A palanquin is a litter carried by servants.
Normally it is a royal conveyance. In this case it was very richly made.

Solomon used the wood of Lebanon – cedar – highly prized for all
kinds of construction for its strength and resistance to decay.

"He made its pillars of silver." The pillars are the uprights that
supported the carrier. They were columns it stood upon that then
extended up to hold a roof or sunshield overhead. It says they were of
silver. I believe they were cedar overlaid with silver, similar to the
construction of the furniture used in the tabernacle.

"Its support of gold." The support of the litter was the base to which the seat and pillars were affixed. It, too, was made of cedar and over-laid with gold to make it both sturdy and beautiful.

"Its seat of purple." Purple was a dye obtained from the shells of a tiny sea creature. It was very rare and highly prized. Only the very rich were able to afford purple. It was usually reserved for royalty.

The vehicle was constructed of the finest materials, but a most impor-tant material mentioned in its construction is the "interior paved with love *for* the daughters of Jerusalem" (The word translated "by" in the NKJV is translated "for" in the KJV).

Hebrews 9:8 and 10:19-23 clearly describe what God means by "a way paved with love." The way into the Holiest of All – the place of unin-hibited fellowship with God – has been "paved with love" for us by the blood of Jesus, our Savior. It is a "new and living way" and we have only to draw near.

There is a skit I once saw on a comedy television show in which a pioneer woman was sweeping the floor of her cabin. She swept and swept with increasing frustration until her husband walked through the door. Whereupon she complained, "I can't get the dirt off this floor." To which he replied, "It's a dirt floor."

I have often thought of that little scene when I have become frustrated with the condition of my heart. I may sweep and sweep at the clay that I am, but I will never come to the end of my humanness. I am made of clay. The amazing thing is this: God likes me this way.

Psalm 103:14 (NKJV) says, "For He knows our frame; He remembers that we are dust." God chose to form us out of the most common material known to man. It is the substance of the earth. We walk upon it. It is the bane of every housewife, yet God made His greatest masterpiece from it. We are clay and God is not surprised by the consistency of the nature we uncover no matter how deeply we may attempt to clean ourselves. We are frail. We are weak. And God has chosen us to display His beauty.

The royal palanquin was made of the wood of Lebanon. Despite this wood's reputation as a preferred construction material, it is still wood. Grown up of the earth – wood in Scripture is a picture of humanness. The king has chosen to make his royal conveyance of wood; in the same way, God has chosen people as the vehicle for His glory to be shown in the earth. His presence is carried by those who are His. Individually and together, we form His royal palanquin.

The wood provides the structure for the vehicle, but it is not seen. It is ornamented and covered, making it a conveyance for the king. Silver is used on the pillars, gold on the base, and purple for the seat; picturing that we are purified, sanctified, and seated in His presence.

I suspect my reader may hold the same attitude I found in my heart – that the wood is the least valuable component in the palanquin. But as I waited before the Lord, I found once again – as so many times I have – that my thinking was opposite to His. The wood is the part given the most importance by Him. That is why He pours out His best on it – His silver, and gold, and purple. Such are we.

As with many types in Scripture, there are varied facets to the palanquin. We can see ourselves as the wood that makes up the structure of the vehicle, but we are also the bride who is seated inside; honored by the king, carried amidst his military strength – protected, cherished, beloved.

I once had a vision of the royal palanquin that quite literally put me on my face before the Lord. I heard the Lord speaking the words, "Wood, silver, gold, purple," repeated like a refrain in my spirit. I took up the words and listened as a heightened awareness of the significance of each of the materials came to me.

God has taken us from glory to glory. We carry the glory of the created in the wood; the glory of the redeemed (bought back from the fall) in the silver; the glory of the sanctified (made holy) in the gold; and the glory of the glorified (seated in heavenly places in Christ Jesus our Lord) in the purple.

He showed me these things, and I worshiped before Him, amazed once again by the condescension of our God. But then the picture panned back, and I saw the thing that laid me out before Him, and from which I hope never to recover. I saw Jesus, bloodied and bent, with a wooden cross upon His back. And upon the cross, bowed low by its weight, Jesus carried the royal palanquin.

All that we are He won for us. The position we enjoy in His presence, Jesus gained for us on the cross. It is all His doing, and it is a finished work. Our part is to accept the place He has made for us and to receive the goodness He gives to us.

A palanquin is a litter carried by servants. The palanquin of the bride is carried by the Servant. Let us not say to Him as Peter did, "Lord, are you washing my feet?" (John 13:6, NKJV). Receiving His ministry is a vital step into intimacy. Allow it to settle in your heart. Allow Him to carry you in His royal coach. Allow Him to serve you as it is in His heart to do.

The joy the bridegroom has in his bride and his lavish love toward her has prompted her words, "Go forth, O daughters of Zion, and see King Solomon with the crown with which his mother crowned him on the day of his wedding, the day of the gladness of his heart" (Song 3:11).

"The day of the gladness of his heart." Astonishing! In Hebrews 12:2, we are told it was for the joy set before Him that Jesus endured the cross, counting the shame as nothing. Jesus walked the path to Calvary with a prize in His mind's eye. He considered that to free His bride from the fall and restore her to oneness with Himself well worth the price. We are His crown, the joy set before Him.

YOU ARE FAIR

"Behold, you are fair, my love! Behold, you are fair! You have dove's eyes behind your veil. Your hair is like a flock of goats, going down from Mount Gilead. Your teeth are like a flock of shorn sheep which have come up from the washing, every one of which bears twins, and none is barren among them. Your lips are like a strand of scarlet, and your mouth is lovely. Your temples behind your veil are like a piece of pomegranate. Your neck is like the tower of David, built for an armory, on which hang a thousand bucklers, all shields of mighty men. Your two breasts are like two fawns, twins of a gazelle, which feed among the lilies" (Song 4:1-5).

In the plan of God, there is a person He formed us each to be. As we live our lives before Him and look into His eyes, the person He sees begins to take shape within our hearts. He speaks and shows us who we are meant to be. It is the eternal one who sees who we truly are. Time does not limit, nor does experience change His vision. We are what He sees. He places His vision within each of our hearts as we draw near and learn to listen to what He says about us.

We may see it as a distant dream at first; but the more we are able to take hold of His vision for our lives, the more we become what He sees when He looks upon us. We are taken from glory to glory, transformed by the words of love and faith spoken by The-One-Who-Sees-And-Loves-Us. What Jesus says about us is what is true. Other people may say one thing; our history and even our own hearts may tell us another; but the only true assessment of who we are belongs to the one who formed us.

This is a kingdom principle: words create. Our Bridegroom is very good at putting before us the words which draw out of us what we are becoming. As He tells us what He sees, our hearts respond with the desire to be as He sees us. The Spirit of Grace then comes and helps us to enter into the truth of who we were created to be.

Here we come to a passage where, from the fullness of his love, the bridegroom pours out words to describe the beauty of his beloved. At first the words are merely hard to understand, but as the meaning becomes clear, the words become difficult to believe.

Once again, it is an act of love toward Jesus to open our hearts and allow His words to penetrate the self-protection and disbelief most of us keep as shields around our souls. To believe what God says about us and to allow it to flow over and fill our beings is our next vital step into intimacy with Him.

The bride has begun to see her bridegroom in a new light. She has trusted him with her heart, with her most closely held secrets, and he has not failed her. She turned to him in absolute vulnerability. He took her to himself and honored her beyond her highest hopes. She was filled with the knowledge of his goodness and saw the impenetrable shield he had placed around her life. The hidden things that had once tormented her have lost their hold in the light of his acceptance.

The threatening things which had made her afraid have lost their power over her. She knows she is safe in his strength, because the one who loves her is the warrior king.

It is in this place of deepening trust between them that the bridegroom describes his beloved. I can imagine the look in his eyes as he gazes at her. The love and the joy he feels shines like sunlight spilling forth, warming her and drawing her in. The love in his eyes quiets the fears in her heart that he may find her lacking or unlovely in any way. She is not yet convinced she is beautiful. She is very deeply in love but isn't sure she is enough to keep his love. He sees this, so he draws her to himself and begins by gazing deeply into her eyes.

He speaks saying, "Behold you are fair, my love! Behold, you are fair! You have dove's eyes behind your veil" (Song 4:1).

"Behold," is the first word from his mouth following the bride's admonition to the daughters of Jerusalem to "go, see" the bridegroom. Her eyes are fixed on him. Her heart is filled with the wonder of his love. She wants only to turn the honor of those around her toward the one who has so captivated her heart, yet his focus is to describe the beauty that is within her.

He says, "Look at you! Just, look at you! You are beautiful, my love. You shine with the radiance of your beauty. Your eyes, so filled with trust toward me, have captured my heart. What is veiled to others is clear to me. I see what is in your heart. Your eyes pour light and love and trust toward me like a fountain of clear water which bubbles up from your soul."

He lifts her veil away, unbinds her hair, and while gently finger-combing the thick dark strands, he whispers, "Your hair is like a flock of goats, going down from Mount Gilead" (Song 4:1). He buries his face in the softness, breathing in her fragrance. The image of the goats on Mt. Gilead speaks of the rippling effect of a flock of little dark-haired goats moving down the side of the mountain, which has often been a place of refuge for the people of God. The bride's hair is a picture of her thoughts; they extend from her head. The image of the goats on Mt. Gilead says that she has learned to put her trust in him. Her thoughts are filled with the comforting knowledge of his loving protection upon her life.

LOVELY MOUTH

The bride smiles and her bridegroom's attention is drawn to her mouth. With a finger beneath her chin, he gently tilts her face upward. Shyly, she bites at her lip. He smiles and says, "Your teeth are like a flock of shorn sheep which have come up from the washing, every one of which bears twins, and none is barren among them" (Song 4:2).

He describes her as having even, white teeth with nothing to detract from the beauty of her smile, but more than that he compares them to sheep.

The irony of describing the bride's teeth as the gentlest and most helpless of creatures is profound. Nearly every other reference to teeth in Scripture compares them to sharp tools or weapons, or speaks of them in reference to the ravaging, devouring animals that use them to consume their prey. Sharp teeth are used as a picture in many of these passages for harsh words spoken by cruel people, and the destructiveness their words work.

But the bride's teeth are compared to sheep. Her words are spoken in the gentleness of wisdom. She speaks with the wisdom from above that James 3:17 says is pure, peaceable, merciful, and true. Her words are not empty, but are filled with truth made palatable by kindness; and the difference they make to those who hear them is the difference between life and death.

The bridegroom expresses his appreciation by saying in effect, "Your words are gentle and filled with kindness. I love the mercy that pours from your mouth. Even at times when you could speak harshly, casting just judgment on those who oppose you, you choose to offer comfort, helping those very ones to come into the way of peace. There is life in all of your words."

The bridegroom continues his perusal of her mouth saying, "Your lips are like a strand of scarlet, and your mouth is lovely" (Song 4:3).

Just as sheep are the animals of redemption, scarlet is the color of redemption. It was a scarlet cord tied to the window of Rahab's home that clued the invading army of Israel that those within were to be spared in the destruction of Jericho (Joshua 2).

Scarlet is the color of blood and has long been associated with atoning sacrifice. Together, teeth of sheep and lips of scarlet describe a mouth that speaks from the heart of God. Jesus, Himself, was the Lamb slain for the sins of the world, and the bride is His voice into the hearts of men until He returns.

The word used to describe the bride's mouth is translated as "lovely." It could also be called pleasant, beautiful, or suitable. But the root of the word means, "to be at home." Oh, to have a mouth where the Lord finds a home! To have lips that speak what He would speak, and teeth that show His mercy. To have a mouth so filled with the words that pour from His heart that we would hear Him say, "Lovely!"

POMEGRANATE THOUGHTS

The bridegroom continues his description of his bride with these words, "Your temples behind your veil are like a piece of pomegranate" (Song 4:3).

Since a pomegranate is a fruit consisting of a leathery rind filled with succulent red seeds, the obvious take on these words is that the bride's thoughts are fruitful. But I could not be satisfied stopping there. As I continued to pray and study this passage, I found pomegranates showing up in the oddest places: around the hem of the high priest's robe, and on the columns of the entrance to the temple.

When we understand that the high priest and the temple symbolically represent the heavenly originals, we must acknowledge that pomegranates represent something very important to God. As was made evident by the woman who touched Jesus' robe and was healed, the very hem of Jesus' garment is laced with fruitfulness, the power to produce life. So, too, the entrance to the residence of our Father is marked with fruitfulness. All who enter are given eternal life.

The first command God gave to both man and animal immediately following their creation was, "Be fruitful and multiply" (Genesis 1:22).

If we ask the question, "What is God like?" The answer must include that God is filled with life, and He is a giver of life.

God made man in His image, investing in the human race the life-giving attributes that so mark and define Him. These attributes were greatly diminished with the fall. For Adam and Eve, both in working the earth and in their own bodies, bringing forth life became a painful and difficult labor. Yet much of the loss from the fall occurred in the mind of man.

As Adam's descendants we have accepted an outlook of life that robs us of our likeness to the one who made us. The Bible speaks of it as a loss of vision, or having a darkened mind. In Paul's letter to the church at Ephesus he stated, "I pray that the eyes of your heart may be enlightened, so that you may know what is the hope of His calling, what are the riches of the glory of His inheritance in the saints, and what is the surpassing greatness of His power toward us who believe" (Ephesians 1:16-19).

The image of fruitfulness in the pomegranate isn't merely in the sweet flesh of the fruit, but in the promise contained in the seeds. This is a fruit made up of seeds contained in individual pouches of juicy pulp and held together in the rind. I know of no other fruit that so emphasizes the seeds. If we think of the seeds as the potential to produce life, we will begin to see what the bridegroom is saying about his beloved's mind.

I believe he is saying her thoughts are pleasing to him. Despite the presence of a veil that caused her to "see through a glass darkly" (1 Corinthians 13:12, KJV) hidden things belong to her. Her thoughts are like a piece of pomegranate filled with the promise of abundant life. Light has come into her mind, and she is taking hold of "the hope of his calling, the riches of the glory of his inheritance in her, and the greatness of his power toward her" (Ephesians 1:18, KJV). The life that is in him is breathing life into her mind. She is learning to agree with her bridegroom for what is true about her, and with that agreement comes the restoration of the promise for the fullness of his life in her.

The light chasing away the darkness in the bride's mind, the flood of truth ushering the essence of heaven into her being, has the bridegroom's heart dancing with joy. His eyes are alight with delight as he looks into her face and says, "Your temples are a piece of pomegranate behind your veil." Or in other words, he says, "Your willingness to believe what you cannot see and join yourself to me is birthing in you the life that is so much a part of me."

DETERMINATION

*N*ow the bridegroom's eyes drop to the column of her throat, slender and strong. It was likely adorned with a necklace of tiny gold medallions strung on chains of fine gold. He says, "Your neck is like the tower of David, built for an armory, on which hang a thousand bucklers, all shields of mighty men" (Song 4:4).

Once again, looking at a contrast for the content of this verse will help us to understand its significance. The bridegroom likens his bride's neck to the tower of David. David built several towers as military strongholds and outposts, but none of them gained fame as the tower of David. David's tower is found in Psalm 144:1-2 (NKJV): "Blessed be the LORD, my Rock . . . my lovingkindness and my fortress, *my high tower,* and my deliverer, my shield and the *One* in whom I take refuge."

Compare David's tower with another famous tower in Genesis 11:4 (NKJV), the tower of Babel. "And they said, 'Come, let us build ourselves a city, and a tower whose top is in the heavens; let us make a name for ourselves, lest we be scattered abroad over the face of the whole earth.'" *Let us make a name for ourselves* is the crux of the matter. The tower was for fame to celebrate their might and accomplishments.

The neck is the part of the body we associate with the human will. Stubbornness is spoken of as being stiff-necked. Compliance is seen in a bowed head, or neck. To put a foot on the enemy's neck is to conquer him, to overrule his will. Laying a yoke on an animal's neck gives the one holding the reins power to direct it, even against its will.

But David was a man whose heart belonged to God so much that his greatest fame is in the words spoken by God, "I have found David the *son* of Jesse, a man after My *own* heart, who will do all My will" (Acts 13:22, NKJV). David was a man whose will was to do the will of God. He was not merely yielded or submitted to God. His will was set – as a strength directed.

David may have been called many things by his enemies, but I am quite sure he was never called "weak." He was a fierce warrior, feared by his enemies. He was the leader of an elite group known as David's mighty men. These were men renowned for their amazing feats of strength and military prowess. Yet David declared time and again throughout the Psalms that his strength was in God. God was his help, his shield, his tower.

Now the bridegroom is describing the bride's neck as being like the tower of David, the place of refuge and safety for this mighty man. What could it mean but that the bride has turned all her heart toward doing the will of God, and has found in this intentional yieldedness the refuge and strength David found?

He says her neck is like the tower of David, built for an armory, on which hang a thousand bucklers, all shields of mighty men. The word for armory is from a word meaning "to tower," as something tall and slender, emphasizing the upward reach of her will toward God.

The thousand bucklers hanging on the tower could be a reference to the practice of taking from among the spoils of battle the shields of kings and other military leaders to hang as trophies on the walls. Or it could be a reference to Solomon's commission to fashion hundreds of shields, some gold, some bronze, to hang on the walls of his houses in order to display his wealth and strength. But I believe it is more likely speaking of the city under siege when the strength of the warriors within is made evident by their shields hanging on the battlements as they position themselves to stand and defend the city. Whichever way you read it, the reference to shields hung on the walls is always a tribute to the military strength within.

A thousand shields hang on this tower. The thousand was the largest military unit in David's army. To speak of the strength of a thousand in human terms is to speak of the strongest fighting force. But thousand has another meaning I think is applicable here. Thousand is a number as a multiple of ten that speaks of righteousness. It is ten times ten times ten. Three is the number for God; the Trinity. Ten to the third power is a reference to the fullness of God's righteousness.

In Isaiah 54:14 (NKJV), we read, "In righteousness you shall be established; You shall be far from oppression, for you shall not fear; And from terror, for it shall not come near you." And in Psalm 71:16 (NKJV), we find, "I will go in the strength of the Lord God; I will make mention of Your righteousness, of Yours only."

The righteousness of God becomes a strength and a shield to those who give themselves to Him. To state that a thousand shields hang upon the tower is to say, "God is in the house!" His righteousness is present to cover and protect, and "terror . . . shall not come near you."

This verse then speaks of the bride's will as not only yielded to the Lord, but turned toward Him in a determined choice to do what pleases Him. This causes her life to be encompassed with the righteousness of God, which is not only a safety to her, but a terror to the enemy of her soul.

The joy in the bridegroom's eyes as he looks at the one who has so chosen to give herself to him is palpable. The words, "Your neck is like the tower of David, built for an armory, on which hang a thousand bucklers, all shields of mighty men," now sound in our hearts as, "Because you have turned your heart toward me to please me in all of your ways, my righteousness has become your fortress, and your heart has found a shelter no enemy can breach."

HEART TO HEART

 ow the bridegroom's eyes come to rest upon two soft mounds nestled beneath draperies of fine white linen, and he says, "Your two breasts are like two fawns, twins of a gazelle, which feed among the lilies" (Song 4:5).

This aspect of the bride's being makes him think of the young of the gentlest and most timid of creatures. Shy and elusive, these creatures of the wild have become the picture for all that is soft and lovely. Their beauty is intriguing, mysterious, enticing; as are the breasts of the bride. The bride's breasts speak of her heart.

The beauty in the bride's soul is intriguing and mysterious. In the same way a deer needs the assurance of safety to rest, the bride needs the assurance of acceptance to allow her heart to be at peace. Two is the number of agreement. The bride's heart is one with her bridegroom's, and her trust is as lovely fawns of the gazelle. He does not take for granted this gift of her trust. The quietness within her gives her bridegroom great satisfaction. The comfort and nurture she finds in trust is a source of deep joy to him.

The bridegroom's heart is overflowing with the beauty of his bride and with the gift of her heart to him. And he says, "The beauty of your soul is as gentle as the deer, as tender as the young of the gazelle. The trust you have given me is as the trust of fawns as they rest and feed among the flowers of the field."

As I come to the end of this passage, I am wondering what it would be like if we were to allow the Lord to lift away the veils we have wrapped around our souls, to remove them as a lover would. What would it do for us to allow Him to unveil our hearts with the awe and appreciation shown to the bride, to truly see the delight shining in His eyes?

I believe in the moments when we are filled with the knowledge that we are deeply and thoroughly loved—when we are aware that we are cherished by The-One-Who-Sees—it settles us. It fills us with contentment and a sense of peace which touches all our interactions with others. We find that we stand up straighter. We lose our shyness, yet do not have to grasp for attention. We can be ourselves with nothing hidden or put on.

The seven attributes of the bride described in this passage do not refer to the fallen state of mankind. They speak of the way we were formed. This is who we are with nothing added or lost. We were created in the imagination of God, and exquisitely fashioned by the one who formed the flowers, the stars, the mountains, the seas; all that we find beautiful in our world. We may wonder at the beauty of the world; yet the truth we need to believe is that of all the beauty the Lord created, He saved His best to put into you and me. We are His masterpiece, His greatest treasure.

Here is a doorway for intimacy with the Lord: that we take God's assessment of ourselves as the measure for who we are. It is found when we look into His eyes to see our reflection there. It is walked out by believing Him as He tells us who we are. Yes, we fall short of His ideal, but He fills up all that is lacking in us and does not chide us for missing what we have yet to come into. Instead, He praises us for every step we take while walking in the pathway He has lit for our feet. This is the doorway. I can only show it to you. Each of us must explore there on our own.

UPWARD

"Until the day breaks and the shadows flee away,
I will go my way to the mountain of myrrh and
to the hill of frankincense" (Song 4:6).

It would be difficult for me to choose one favorite verse from the Song, but this one is in my top three. This little verse has been like a brilliant light shining on my path in some of the darkest days of my life. The innate hope within these words has been a lifeline I have clung to while awaiting the word on medical tests and as I was slogging my way back to health from a difficult illness. This verse shows me how to approach a day filled with storm clouds and uncertainty. Encapsulated in these words is the key to living in the peace of God.

"Until the day breaks and the shadows flee away" speaks of the night. Night can refer to the natural ebbing of the light which comes at the end of a day. The ebb and flow of light is as natural as that of the tide. Night follows day. Spiritual ebbs and flows happen as well. There are days when light is abundant, joy is easy, and there are no shadows or uncertainty. And there are nights when it is hard to see, when darkness hides the colors, and all is quiet and dim. But night can also be a time of struggle, of testing, of sadness, or of fear.

During a time of darkness, the bride states she will go her way to the mountain of myrrh. To say she will "go her way" is to declare a choice, an act of her will. The place she goes in the dark of night is to the mountain of myrrh and the hill of frankincense.

"The mountain of myrrh . . ." A mountain is a place of strength and surety, as a natural fortress or stronghold of protection. Myrrh is a primary ingredient in the holy oil used to anoint the tabernacle and its furnishings. It was also used to anoint the priests who served the Lord in the tabernacle. Myrrh is a sign of consecration. To be consecrated is to be set apart and marked for a single and specific purpose.

Jesus was given myrrh at His birth and anointed with myrrh at His death. In living and in dying, His life was wholly God's. Consecration of our hearts to God is done by making a choice to entrust every aspect of our lives to Him regardless of our feelings or circumstances.

"The hill of frankincense . . ." A hill is a place of high elevation; a place to go that rises above the plain. It is a place of revelation and fellowship with God. Frankincense was also used in the tabernacle worship. It was a key ingredient in the incense which was offered daily before the Lord in the holy place. Morning and evening, the high priest burned the incense on the altar before the ark of the testimony, and the Lord met him there. Frankincense speaks of acceptable prayer offered to and received by God. Acceptable prayer is prayer that is in agreement with the heart of God.

Frankincense was also one of the gifts given to Jesus by the Magi; signifying His life would be an acceptable sacrifice, a pleasing aroma to God. We join the Lord on the hill of frankincense when we come to Him to pour out our hearts in love and thanksgiving simply because He is worthy. I have often felt the incense of my praise was sweetest to the Lord when I pushed past my fears and gave Him my love and trust at times when the darkness was heaviest around me.

In this passage, the bride declares that through the night she watches and waits for the dawn. While she waits, she directs her soul to trust in the one who will not fail her; she makes her way to the mountain of myrrh. But she doesn't just fall on her face brokenly pleading for his intervention; she instructs her soul to give thanks; she goes to the hill of frankincense. She waits, without telling him what the outcome should be. She silences the voices which arise to tell her to be afraid that his heart is not for her; his eyes are not on her. She overrules the clamoring of her soul with the giving of thanks until her soul comes into agreement with the one who loves her.

The bride's words, "Until the day breaks and the shadows flee away I will go my way to the mountain of myrrh and to the hill of frankincense" mean to me, "Throughout the dark and fearsome night, when confusion and uncertainty surround me, I make the choice to lay my heart before the Lord and place my life in His nail-scarred hands. I will trust Him when I am afraid. While I wait for the morning sun, I turn toward Him with the praise of my heart. I choose to give thanks to the Lord. Though night surrounds me and all about me is dark, I will quiet my heart and wait, for the dawn will surely come. When the storm rages, I entrust my life to the one who hides me in God. Darkness cannot hurt me when I am in Jesus. He is my Mountain of Myrrh and my Hill of Frankincense."

Dear friend, here is an open door for you. When the darkness presses around you and the voice of fear sounds loudly in your ears, I encourage you to take yourself to the Mountain of Myrrh and the Hill of Frankincense. We enter by exercising our will to give thanks to the one Who died for us. Do you have nothing for which to thank Him? If you are breathing air, that is a place to start. If you have water to drink, if you can see the sky, a flower, a bird—give thanks. Set yourself to begin, and you will soon see how much there is to be thankful for.

Then, by an act of your will, lay your life in His hands. If all you are able to do is say, "I want to trust you, but I am afraid," begin with that. He will help you. Ask Him for a verse of Scripture or a picture to help you to enter more deeply into rest. I promise you, God will never fault you if you need help to draw near to Him. The prodigal's father *ran* to him as soon as he saw his son on the horizon. Our Father is passionate in His desire to have us with Him. Be assured He will help you as often and as much as you need it. He *knows* we need Him. It is only on our side that we struggle to be independent of His help. He designed us to be in complete union with Him. He has always intended to fill every need in our hearts.

YOU ARE ALL FAIR

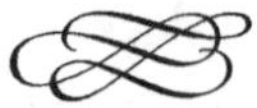

efore we go on, I would like to draw your attention to a similar passage from chapter two of the Song. At that time, the bride was speaking in response to the bridegroom's entreaty to join him on the mountains. She said, "My beloved is mine and I am his. He feeds his flock among the lilies. Until the day breaks and the shadows flee away, turn my beloved and be like a gazelle or a young stag upon the mountains of Bether."

If you will recall, it was the bride's attitude then that she was content with the safety and comfort of her situation. She was happy to join her bridegroom in the places she had grown accustomed to seeing him. Feeding the flock among the lilies speaks of the contentment and rest of her soul. The mountains in this passage were called "separation." She saw the mountains as beyond her abilities and didn't mind passing up the opportunity of going there since she expected nothing else would change. But something did change, and it required her to change as well.

The bridegroom withdrew, and she was forced to go out and find him in the night. When she found him, she brought him to her mother's house and gave him access to the foundations of her life; the hidden places that had shaped her perspectives on life and herself. His response was to take her to the wilderness and spend time with her there. While there and upon their return, the bride began to see a facet of her bridegroom, which opened her heart to a new level of trust toward him and a deeper confidence in his love for her.

She saw his strength and commitment to her; and she saw what he had done to draw her into his love. When darkness came, she refused to let her thoughts betray her trust in him. She waited for him with her heart laid out as an offering; and while she waited, she spoke of the goodness of her bridegroom and gave thanks.

This gift of the bride's love and trust in the night prompts one of the most moving passages in the Song. The bridegroom begins this passage by praising his bride with, "You are all fair, my love, and there is no spot in you." In his delight, he takes her with him to explore the mountains which had once so intimidated her. Then he goes on to describe what her love means to him in some of the most beautiful words ever written. The bridegroom declares:

> "You are all fair, my love, and there is no spot in you.
> Come with me from Lebanon, my spouse, with me from
> Lebanon. Look from the top of Amana, from the top
> of Senir and Hermon, from the lion's dens,
> from the mountains of the leopards.

> "You have ravished my heart, my sister, my
> spouse; you have ravished my heart with one
> look of your eyes, with one link of your necklace.
> How fair is your love, my sister, my spouse! How
> much better than wine is your love, and the scent
> of your perfumes than all spices! Your lips, O my
> spouse, drip as the honeycomb; Honey and milk
> are under your tongue; and the fragrance of your
> garments is like the fragrance of Lebanon.

> "A garden enclosed is my sister, my spouse, a
> spring shut up, a fountain sealed. Your plants are
> an orchard of pomegranates with pleasant fruits,
> fragrant henna with spikenard, spikenard and
> saffron, calamus and cinnamon, with all trees of
> frankincense, myrrh and aloes, with all of the
> chief spices – a fountain of gardens, a well of living
> waters, and streams from Lebanon" (Song 4:7-14).

"You are all fair, my love, there is no spot in you," begins the bridegroom in his outpouring of praise for the bride. The bride has taken herself to the mountain of myrrh to dwell in the strength of his shadow through the night. She has remained in quiet trust and thankfulness in the hill of frankincense while darkness shrouded her life. She has learned to take herself to the rest and safety of her bridegroom's arms through the uncertainty of life, and he declares over her that she is all fair. There is no spot to be found in her.

I cannot help but wonder if Paul was thinking of this passage in the Song when he wrote to the Ephesians, describing the love of Christ for His church. In Ephesians 5:25-27 (NKJV), we read, ". . . Christ . . . loved the church and gave Himself for her, that He might sanctify and cleanse her with the washing of water by the word, that He might present her to Himself a glorious church, not having spot or wrinkle or any such thing, but that she should be holy and without blemish."

The love of Jesus, trustingly believed and received, bathes the bride in holiness, making her glorious. Through His gift of life, she is all fair. In the eyes of her beloved, there is no memory of wrong. She is without spot.

Once again, I would encourage my reader to let these words go into your heart and work their transforming power in your life. I remember the first time I heard the whispered words of my Lord saying, "You are all fair, my love." I wept with the pain of my failures. I knew it was impossible for me to allow Him to see me as "fair," and yet I wanted so much to be beautiful to Him. I reminded Him of all the ways that I knew it couldn't be true. Yet He whispered once again, "You are fair. There is no spot in you."

Then I knew the choice was mine to make. I could believe what He declared and move into deeper intimacy with Him; or I could maintain my belief in my unfitness and stand apart from the place He was opening before me in His arms. He speaks - then He waits, holding His arms wide, until we dare to move into them and allow ourselves to be enfolded more deeply in His love. The choice to believe and take the next step is always our own.

A MOUNTAIN CALLED LEBANON

"Come with me from Lebanon, my spouse,
with me from Lebanon, look from the top of Amana,
from the top of Senir and Hermon, from the lions' dens,
from the mountains of the leopards" (Song 4:8).

*L*ebanon is a mountainous region to the north of Israel made up of two mountain ranges and a river valley. Mt. Hermon is the highest peak in the Anti-Lebanon Range rising over 9,000 feet above sea-level. Snow-capped year round, often shrouded in fog and rain, the mountain is the source of much of the valley's moisture. The many springs and streams emerging at the base of the mountain supply life-giving water to this arid land.

Mt. Hermon, also called Senir or Sirion, is a triple-peaked mountain. The three mountains named in the verse are likely three peaks of the same mountain. The word Hermon comes from a root word in the Hebrew meaning "to seclude or devote to religious uses, to consecrate." The mountain was considered a holy place. Many sites of worship have been discovered there, both pagan and Hebrew. Amana means "covenant." It comes from the same root from which we get our word Amen, which means "a truth," or "so be it." Senir means "to be pointed, a peak."

Cedar forests covered much of the mountain range and were renowned for both their beauty and desirability as a building material. These trees were used to build the temple and the king's palace. The forests also provided a home for wildlife. Great cats, bears, and deer, as well as many smaller animals found abundant cover and provision deep in the forests of Lebanon.

The word Lebanon means "white." The name is derived from the snow-capped peaks which crown the region. But the word comes from a Hebrew root which means "heart," referring to the most interior organ of the body, to the breast, or to courage or understanding.

With these things in mind, let's look again at this verse. "Come with me from Lebanon, my spouse," encourages the bridegroom, "with me from Lebanon. Look from the top of Amana, from the top of Senir and Hermon, from the lions' dens, from the mountains of the leopards."

This is the first time the bridegroom calls the bride his spouse. The word has the meaning "bride," but it is from a root which means "to complete or make perfect." Something has changed. The bride has moved into a different place in their relationship than she had occupied before. Somehow, through all that has happened, she has come into a place in his heart which completes him. She now fills a place in him she alone can be.

The bridegroom says, "Come with me from Lebanon . . ." He is not asking that she go with him *to* Lebanon. He repeats, "Come with me," emphasizing they are already together in this place of the highest peaks in the deepest wilderness of the land. Lions and leopards dwell in the forest. Images of these cats adorn thrones and palaces. As symbols of royalty, they were captured and kept as pets in the royal courts of the day. The bridegroom is inviting his spouse to explore the wildness and majesty of Lebanon.

Almost without being aware of when or how it happened, she has come to this covenant place (Amana), this holy mountain (Senir), this sanctuary (Hermon). Here, the bridegroom extends his hand to the one who completes him, asking her to inhabit the deepest places of his heart. She has gained entrance to a place few ever see. It is the bridegroom's desire that she come with him to take in the beauty and breathe in the air, leaving her scent and presence on the mountain, even as the scent and presence of the mountain fills and surrounds her.

When we last saw the bride, she had taken herself to the mountain of myrrh and to the hill of frankincense to await the dawn. (Myrrh is for consecration which is seen in trust. Frankincense is for worship which is shown by love). The bride waited on the mountain for the night to pass, and while she waited, she offered to her bridegroom her love and her trust.

Love and trust became her guides as she waited for the morning sun. It was they that held her hands, keeping her joined to the one she loved when she stumbled in the darkness. Though unaware of his nearness, his goodness refreshed her when weariness and despair threatened to overwhelm her. Deeper into the wilderness she journeyed through the night.

Perhaps she had gone to the mountain in fear and sorrow; yet now, as the shadows lift, she looks about in the glimmering light as one awakening from a long and heavy slumber. Love and life surround her, pulsing with eager joy. Where is the terror of the night? Where is the despair? All that surrounds her now is the immediacy of his presence defining her world.

Astonishment fills her heart as she looks at her beloved. She remembers the faltering steps, the questions, the doubts that assailed her through the night. Small and frail though they were, her love and trust led her here. Now, in the dawning light, she looks at the vistas which lie at her feet. The darkness has fled. She fills her lungs with the air of Lebanon, breathing in liberty to her soul. She seems to be at the top of the world, even to be "seated in heavenly places" (Ephesians 2:6) far above all of the struggle and pain in the valley below. She is beginning to see she has left the realm she once inhabited and has come to dwell in a kingdom far above the rule and authority of that world.

YOU HAVE RAVISHED MY HEART

As the dawn lights the world around her, the bride turns to her bridegroom with wonder and love shining in her eyes. He draws her hand into his, cradling it against his breast as she moves into his embrace. He whispers, "You have ravished my heart, my sister, my spouse; you have ravished my heart with one look of your eyes, with one link of your necklace" (Song 4:9). Ravished is a word which literally means to be enclosed, or captured, but it shares the same Hebrew root as Lebanon which means 'heart.' "You have ravished my heart" could be said, "You have taken my heart captive."

He calls her "My sister, my spouse . . ." We have already talked about the significance of the word 'spouse,' as the one who completes him. But why would he say *my sister*? The word is the feminine word for 'kindred.' It is used to suggest one who has a similar affinity or is like-minded.

As I speak of this passage, I must pause and tell you that in wonderment at these words, I asked God, "How can this be? How can it be real that my small and imperfect love can draw such a response from you?" His answer to me was simply, "It is all I have ever wanted."

Most of us expect God to be unwilling to extend kindness to us. We try to please Him so He will care for us. We dread His anger, expect harsh dealing from Him, and look for ways to shield ourselves from Him. We think His kindness is limited and His love is given in response to our good behavior. This is often quite unconscious, yet the truth of it is seen in our astonishment and disbelief when we are confronted with Scripture such as this, "You have ravished my heart, my sister, my spouse; you have ravished my heart with one glance of your eyes, with one link of your necklace."

Here is a glimpse into the heart of God. Please, for a moment, try to leave your struggle to believe His kindness and generosity. Lay it down as you look into this portal. Come and see His love for you.

"You have ravished My heart . . ." Literally He says, "You have stripped my heart of its coverings. You have taken my heart captive and it now belongs to you."

"My sister, my spouse . . ."

"You are of my own likeness, designed and suited to be my match. You fit me. You fulfill me."

"You have ravished My heart with one glance of your eyes, with one link of your necklace."

"So completely does My heartbeat for you, that the love that shines so trustingly in your eyes and the choice of your heart to turn toward me has captivated me. I am undone."

The bridegroom continues, "How fair is your love, my sister, my spouse! How much better than wine is your love, and the scent of your perfumes than all spices!" (Song 4:10). In other words, he says, "How beautiful is your love, my sister-spouse. It is intoxicating. Your love is sweeter to me than all good things!"

"Your lips, O my spouse, drip as the honeycomb; honey and milk are under your tongue; and the fragrance of your garments is like the fragrance of Lebanon" (Song 4:11). Rich and fertile land is described as a land flowing with milk and honey; a land abundant in the things which sustain life. The air of Lebanon has bathed the bride in cedar and sunshine and the rich scents of the forest. Just as the scent of spikenard undoubtedly clung to Mary's hair following her anointing of Jesus, so now the scent which identifies the bridegroom, the fragrance of Lebanon, clings to the bride as well. The bridegroom says, "Sweetness and goodness fill your mouth. Your very garments carry the fragrance of my heart."

Do you remember the opening words of the bride in the Song? She described the bridegroom's love as intoxicating and spoke of his scent as that which filled her with desire to pursue him, to be drawn away with him. Now the bridegroom uses these same words to describe his feelings for his bride.

Standing on the mountain in the dawning light, the bridegroom looks at this woman who has trusted him in the darkness. This woman who now turns to him with the undemanding love of one whose heart is set to give him all that she has without reserve. In her eyes, fathoms deep, he sees the purity of her heart. Her trust is his treasure. It overwhelms him and gives him strength. He feels invincible and overcome. Her love is intoxicating. Of all that is pleasing and good, her scent is the perfume he most desires. Her love permeates the air around him and fills his heart with the joy of her presence.

Some may argue this cannot be a right interpretation of this verse. They may say God needs nothing from us. He is all powerful; therefore, it is not possible for the love of His people to give Him strength.

I agree God is Almighty. I agree there is nothing we can bring to Him that will add to His consequence or ability. But I have discovered to my great amazement that God has limited Himself in such a way as to make room for what He has put within us. It is the wonder of our redemption that God has so formed and gifted mankind that we carry within us the ability to give love to God. This love is something He will not demand of us; but when we give it, it is His greatest treasure.

God has also put within mankind the ability to discover how to relate to Him by understanding how we relate to one another. Love calls forth strength and courage in men. A man who loves unhesitatingly defends, protects, and provides for those who are his. I have seen this courage and determination displayed by my father, my husband, and my sons. This is an attribute of the nature of God within men.

I have also discovered how the love and trust of a woman strengthens a man's courage and determination. It is not that the man is weak and she makes him strong, nor that he is cowardly and she makes him brave, but her love brings a dimension to his soul which increases his capacity to do what it is within him to do.

Always when I study Scripture, I look for the application to my life. I want to know, "How does this truth affect me?" I know my love adds nothing to God's Person. He is who He is. I am very grateful that He does not change and is not affected by the caprices of mankind. But I think we may see how it can be true that the love we give to God affects His ability to give to us what He desires to give.

Jesus said many times it was the faith of a person which gave Him the freedom to do what was in His heart to do. Did their faith make His abilities miraculous? No. He is who He is. But their faith gave His miraculous power entrance into their lives.

This freedom to act is the power of love. This is the invincibility found by the bridegroom in the trust of his beloved. She has ravished his heart with one look of her eyes, with one link of her necklace. The love and trust she turns toward him has taken his heart captive. Her love has so intoxicated him that to be near her, to breathe her scent, is what he most desires.

Could it be our Bridegroom also finds in the love we give to Him such a treasure? Could it be that, as we turn toward Him in quiet confidence and faith, all that He is by-way-of power and ability stands, awaiting His direction? I only know this: when I see my Lord this way, I want with all my heart to trust Him. I want to give Him all of my love. I don't want to fail Him or withhold anything in my response that His love deserves.

IN YEARNING AND HOPE I OFFER MY HEART TO HIM AND PRAY:

Come, Holy Spirit. Breathe on me. I wait for you. Jesus, you are so much more than I know. Please help me to make room for all you want to be to me. Please open my heart and my mind to the truth that will take me from glory to glory. I worship you, but it is not your greatness, your majesty, or your power that causes me to love you. I know so little of the heights of these. I glimpse but a tiny portion of your greatness. Truly, you are a great God; King, and Lord above all. I honor you, but my heart is yours because of the love you give to me.

Your tenderness and understanding; your kindness, gentleness, and patience. Your acceptance and forgiveness have been steadfast and unwavering. I have learned to depend upon your love. I know you love me. I know it all the way through me. Your love has taught me to love you, too. This is my doorway into God. Not your greatness, not your supremacy, not your holiness; but the love you have shown me has invited me to know you.

As I stand on the mountain and survey my world, I raise my eyes and see in the distance far ranges rising through clouds, suggesting other heights to climb, other peaks to explore in the knowledge of God. I feel curiosity about them and hope someday to experience their grandeur and discover their secrets, but for now I am too much occupied to leave my mountain. I have only begun to explore this mountain called Lebanon, the mountain of your heart. I have only just awakened to its marvels. It will be long before I seek another scent to fill my lungs, another view to fill my vision, so captivated am I in your love.

A GARDEN ENCLOSED

The wind whispers and stirs around the couple
as the bridegroom holds his beloved against his
beating heart and says, "A garden enclosed is my
sister, my spouse, a spring shut up, a fountain sealed.
Your plants are an orchard of pomegranates
with pleasant fruits" (Song 4:12-13).

"A garden enclosed . . . a spring shut up, a fountain sealed." A garden is a cultivated piece of ground often fenced or hedged, planted with vegetables and fruits. Royal gardens are filled with rare and beautiful plants which are grown simply for the pleasure of the king. The garden which is the bride is seen as a walled place and her water sources are not free flowing. This is but a place for her to begin. The bridegroom now describes the potential for fruitfulness in her and as she comes to see what he sees within her a dramatic change takes place.

The bridegroom says, "You do not know what is in you. You truly do not understand the potential that is resident within you. You are like a private garden. You have described yourself as an uncared-for vineyard, and as a flower growing commonly in the field where it soon shrivels and dies from lack of moisture or is trampled beneath the hooves of beasts. But the truth is you are cherished and protected. You are a well of joy to your bridegroom. The verdancy and fruitfulness within you has been brought under my guardianship. Soon you will see my promise in the tiny beginnings which you once considered insignificant."

He says, "Your tiny plants are an orchard of pomegranates" (Song 4:13). Pomegranates are a fruit filled with seeds. The bride has counted herself as small and unimportant, but she has within her the potential to produce greatness. The beginnings of life within her may seem as insignificant as a tiny seed, but they are as filled with life-giving power as an orchard of pomegranate trees. Each seed contains within it the ability to produce a tree. Each fruit contains many seeds. Each tree produces many seed-filled fruits every season. The greatness within her is as infinite as Abraham's seed, "as countless as the stars" (Genesis 15:5) beyond the ability to number.

"With pleasant fruits . . ." (Song 4:13). Pleasant means to be eminent or distinguished. The fruit within the bride is an incomparable treasure. Who is qualified to judge the value of a life? Should not God have that privilege? Should not His assessment of our value overrule our own?

"Come, my precious one," our Bridegroom breathes, "lean into my arms and believe. You are my treasure. You are filled with all that is most delightful."

GIFTS

*W*hat can be found in the garden that is the bride? "Fragrant henna . . ." (Song 4:13).

Henna or camphire is a fragrant white flower, producing a reddish dye when crushed, which was used in cosmetics. The root word in the Hebrew means, "a redemption price or ransom." We saw in a previous passage where the bride likened her bridegroom to a cluster of henna in the vineyards of En Gedi. Now the bridegroom is saying the bride carries within her the same sweet fragrance, the same lovely flower capable of imparting beauty and covering sin wherever she goes. Could this be?

John records an instance following Jesus' resurrection from the dead when He came and stood in the midst of the assembled disciples, breathed on them, and said, "Receive the Holy Spirit. If you forgive the sins of any, they are forgiven them; if you retain the sins of any, they are retained" (John 20:22b-23, NKJV).

In 2 Corinthians 5:18-19 (NKJV) Paul states, "Now all things *are* of God, who has reconciled us to Himself through Jesus Christ, and has given us the ministry of reconciliation, that is, that God was in Christ reconciling the world to Himself, not imputing their trespasses to them, and has committed to us the word of reconciliation."

The beauty of henna is seen in sins covered, and trespasses forgiven. This is something we readily attribute to Christ, but it has also been given to the bride to carry Christ's redemptive love to all who seek freedom from sin. The bride carries within her the sweet scent of henna, imparting the fragrance of forgiveness and the beauty of reconciliation wherever she goes.

Next he says, "With spikenard, spikenard . . ." Spikenard is an aromatic ointment made from the sap of the nard plant. It is a perfume - very rare, very costly. In every instance of its use in Scripture, it is seen as something which belongs uniquely to the bride and is associated with the outpouring of her love upon the one she loves. This is what can be seen in Mary's act of adoration when she anointed Jesus with spikenard prior to His crucifixion.

In this passage spikenard is repeated. It is the only plant in the bride's garden that is so emphasized. It is as if the mention of spikenard is so sweet to the bridegroom that he cannot say it only once.

"There is spikenard in the garden." The bridegroom pauses, closes his eyes, inhales, sighs, "Yes, spikenard. Mm. Happy thought. She loves me - loves me."

"And saffron . . ." (Song 4:14). Saffron is a pungent, bright orange spice which comes from the dried stigmas of the crocus flower. In our culture saffron is mostly used in very small quantities to flavor food. But in the biblical world, saffron was recognized and highly regarded for its many healing properties. It was used to treat everything from fevers, coughs, and insect bites to leprosy, gastric ailments, heart conditions, alcoholism, and mental disorders. This lovely, fragrant flower filled with healing abilities is found within the bride.

Healing belongs to the bride. There are many passages to support this, but one that comes immediately to mind is the time Jesus told the Gentile woman who asked Him to heal her child that healing was "the children's bread" (Mark 7:27). In another place Jesus said, "For the bread of God is He who comes down from heaven and gives life to the world." (John 6:33) and He goes on to say, "I am the bread of life" (John 6:35). Jesus gives Himself to the bride. Healing is integral to His gift.

When Jesus sent His disciples out to preach the good news of the kingdom, He told them to "Heal the sick, cleanse the lepers, raise the dead, cast out demons" (Matthew 10:8a, NKJV). The presence of saffron in the garden is a clear promise of the power present with the bride to heal all kinds of diseases.

CALAMUS

"*C*alamus . . ." (Song 4:14). Calamus or sweet cane is an aromatic grass, a reed. It was used in the biblical world in the making of incense and perfumes. In Scripture it is seen as a valuable trade item. It is one of the five ingredients used to make the anointing oil used in the tabernacle (Exodus 30:23).

The Hebrew word for calamus is "qaneh." In Ezekiel 40 "qaneh" is translated as 'measuring rod.' In the next three chapters we see the measuring rod, which is six cubits in length, used over and over to reveal the dimensions of the temple being shown in a vision to the prophet.

Ezekiel describes the cubit as the measure of a man's forearm, elbow to fingertips, plus the width of his hand. God has promised that our lives are held in the palm of His hand, and He measures the length of our days. This measuring is part of His covenant with us. It speaks of His design, His foreknown intention toward us and the surety with which He works out His purposes in our lives.

Sometimes when we study Scripture the most obscure passages reveal the greatest treasures. When I first looked at calamus, I could find nothing very intriguing about it, but I couldn't understand why God would use it in the anointing oil and include it in the bride's garden if there was no more to it than a sweet fragrance. I have long loved the passage in Ezekiel describing the dimensions of the temple, and the picture of God's covenant relationship with us in the description recorded there. When I discovered the measuring rod was the same word for calamus found in the garden, I began to see why it was so important to include this element in His description of the bride.

The presence of calamus in the garden is a sign that God has measured our lives and ordered our days. Our lives may be as fragile as the grass of the field, yet the God of the universe has given us an eternal place within Himself. We are never beyond the reach of His arm or outside the palm of His hand.

The bridegroom looks at his bride and sees calamus. It is a picture of the covenant he has made with her. Calamus in the garden is a symbol of the Lord's promise to come to us, to fill us with His presence and dwell with us forever.

> "As for man, his days are like grass; As a flower of the field, so
> he flourishes. For the wind passes over it, and it is gone.
> And its place remembers it no more. But the mercy of the Lord
> *is* from everlasting to everlasting on those who fear Him,
> and His righteousness to children's children,
> To such as keep His covenant . . ." (Psalm 103:15-18, NKJV).

CINNAMON, MYRRH, AND ALOES

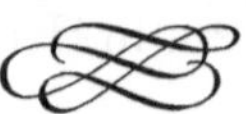

"*And* cinnamon . . ." (Song 4:14). In the biblical world the only sources for cinnamon were the island of Ceylon and the coast of India. Cinnamon was an exotic and costly spice, an important commodity in trade, valued at 25 times its weight in silver. It was used as a sweetener for foods, and in cosmetics and perfumes. Its medicinal properties made it useful in treating various ailments. It was also used to preserve meats and was one of the embalming spices.

Cinnamon points to the promised redemption of our bodies as

> ". . . we groan within ourselves, eagerly waiting for the adoption, the redemption of our body" (Romans 8:23, NKJV).

Cinnamon is fragrant and attractive. To describe the bride as a garden with cinnamon says she is beautiful, irresistible, sought after, and destined for life everlasting.

"With all trees of frankincense . . ." As we have already discovered, frankincense is an important element in worship. It is a gum resin gathered from succulent plants which grow in arid and remote regions of Africa. The resin is obtained by incising the trunks of the trees and allowing the white sap to flow out and harden. It produces a fragrant white smoke when crushed and cast over coals. Frankincense speaks of the purity of a heart poured out in love and thankfulness. It is a necessary element in the bride's garden.

"Myrrh," also has an important place in worship. It was used in anointing oil to signify consecration to God. Articles and people anointed with the oil of myrrh are wholly God's. Myrrh is gathered in much the same way as frankincense. The resin it produces is a reddish-brown gum, which is bitter in scent and taste. It was also used in cosmetics, in embalming, and in medicine as a sedative and pain reliever. Myrrh speaks of a heart filled with trust.

"And aloes . . ." Aloe is called the "medicine plant." Its healing properties in the biblical world were well known and highly regarded. It was used to treat many diseases both externally and internally. Aloe was also used in cosmetics and as an aromatic balm. The presence of both saffron and aloe in the garden indicates that healing for every kind of disease and illness belongs to the bride.

Cinnamon, myrrh, and aloes were used in combination to anoint a person or place in preparation for lovemaking. Psalm 45 refers to these three as the oil of gladness that scents the bridegroom's garments. In typical counterfeit style, the harlot of Proverbs 7 prepares her bed with this combination of spices. The bride's garden has these three elements in abundance. She is anointed and ready for the giving and receiving of love. I believe this combination of spices represents the irresistible combination of sweetness, trust, and innocence in the heart of the bride.

"With all of the chief spices . . ." finishes the list of what was to be found in the bride's garden. All that is most rare and beautiful, most sought after and desired; these are found in the garden that is the bride.

A FOUNTAIN OF GARDENS

"A fountain of gardens, a well of living waters,
and streams from Lebanon" (Song 4:15).

"**A** fountain of gardens" declares the is a source of many gardens. She is capable of reproducing the life in her and can give birth to those who will become gardens equal in beauty and verdancy to her own. "Adam called his wife's name Eve, because *she was the mother of all living*" (Genesis 3:20, NKJV, *emphasis mine*).

"A well of living waters . . ." Wells were deep pits dug to collect and retain water. The water held in them was still - it lacked movement and often became stagnant over time - but living water speaks of flowing water that is being constantly renewed. This well, although deep and hidden, has a source of water that is fresh and flowing.

When Jesus spoke with the woman at the well, He said, "If you knew the gift of God, and who it is who says *to* you, 'Give Me a drink,' you would have asked Him, and He would have given you *living water*. The woman said to Him, 'Sir, You have nothing to draw with, and the well is deep. Where then do you get that living water?' . . . Jesus answered, 'Whoever drinks of this water will thirst again, but whoever drinks of the water that I shall give him will never thirst. But the water that I shall give him will become in him *a fountain of water springing up into everlasting life*'" (John 4:10-14, NKJV, *emphasis mine*).

"Streams from Lebanon . . ." Fresh and pure, the water in this garden finds its source in the mountains of Lebanon, the heart of the bridegroom. Jesus said, ". . . If anyone thirsts, *let him come to Me and drink. He who believes in Me, as the Scripture has said, out of his heart will flow rivers of living water. But this He spoke concerning the Spirit, whom those believing in Him would receive*" (John 7:37-39a, NKJV, *emphasis mine*).

With these things in mind, let us look again at the words of the bridegroom. He says, "A garden enclosed is my sister, my spouse, a spring shut up, a fountain sealed. Your plants are an orchard of pomegranates with pleasant fruits, fragrant henna with spikenard, spikenard and saffron, calamus and cinnamon, with all trees of frankincense, myrrh and aloes, with all the chief spices – a fountain of gardens, a well of living waters, and streams from Lebanon" (Song 4:12-15).

When we last saw the bride and bridegroom, they were standing together on the mountain enjoying the majesty of Lebanon. As the bride moved into her lover's embrace and laid her head against his beating heart, he described how deeply her love and trust affected him. Her scent is the fragrance he loves above all others and the sweetness of her lips and mouth is nourishment to his soul. But he realizes as he holds her there that she doesn't understand who she is. So, he says, "You are like a hidden garden, and within you is a covered spring, a sealed fountain."

She lifts her head and looks wonderingly into his eyes. He smiles tenderly, gently caresses her face, and says, "Yet you are so much more than you have seen or understood. The tiny shoots within your garden are an orchard of pomegranates. Limitless fruitfulness is within you. Though the dreams of your heart have been stunted and squelched, though your wishes have gone mostly unexplored, infinite potential is present with you. Your dreams are not foolishness. Your hopes are not useless. I have given you dreams to dream. I have filled you with wishes and hopes. These are evidence of my presence breathing, speaking, drawing you into the greatness I have always planned for you."

The bride frowns in confusion, trying to understand. The bridegroom sighs and draws her back into his embrace as he continues, "Do not discount the value of your life. Everything I love the most is within you. The mercy I have shown to you has rooted, grown, and blossomed into fragrant white flowers which are now ready to show mercy to others. I have put within you the ability to forgive. In this, your heart is coming into likeness with mine."

The bride looks up and smiles. Her bridegroom smiles at her and says, "The scent of your love for me mingles with the fragrance of forgiveness. Yes, your love joins mine in healing power to touch broken hearts, troubled minds, and hurting bodies. I love the way you are available to do with me the things I long to do. Your willingness to give mercy and love, to offer forgiveness and healing even to those who have wounded you, is the fragrance of the most precious of perfumes; a soul poured out to me in love."

The bridegroom looks once again into his bride's eyes. In the depths of her soul, he sees the hope and promise within her. To see the calamus within her is to see the end from the beginning. He has always known this would be so. She belongs to him. She is the one designed and formed to complete and fulfill the deepest longings of his heart. Once again, he enfolds her into his arms. He inhales the lovely scent surrounding them and says, "Your love, your faith in my goodness, your trust in my kindness, your sweetness and innocence are a balm that brings joy to my heart. I have found in you the treasure I most desire."

The bridegroom continues, "Instead of the hidden, covered, and restricted life you have come to accept, the abundance you are finding in me will offer hope to multitudes. Deep wisdom and understanding will flow through you as a pure stream of water. Its source is my own heart. My life will flow out through you into a dry and thirsty world."

AWAKEN THE WIND

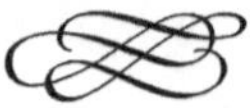

The bridegroom's words cause the bride to respond, "Awake, O north wind, and come, O south! Blow upon my garden that its spices may flow out. Let my beloved come to his garden and eat its pleasant fruits" (Song 4:16).

The north wind carries the cold air of winter; the south brings the warm breezes of summer. In winter the seeds drop to the ground, and the trees lay dormant, resting before the growing season to come. In winter, plants gain strength and resiliency. Then, when the warm breezes breathe upon the garden, the sap begins to flow. The seeds awaken and sprout into newness of life. The trees bud and blossom. The garden bursts forth into new life. The bride understands that the wonder of springtime doesn't happen without winter. Both are needed for fruitfulness.

Wind also represents the presence of the Holy Spirit. In the second chapter of Acts, the Holy Spirit came with the sound of a rushing, mighty wind.

When Gabriel came to Mary to announce that by the overshadowing of the Holy Spirit the Savior would be born through her, her surrendered heart responded, "Let it be to me according to your word" (Luke 1:38, NKJV).

When the bride says, "Awake, O north wind, and come, O south," I hear her answering with the same heart that was in Mary, "Come, Holy Spirit! Perform what God has spoken. Breathe upon my garden that its spices may flow out. Do whatever is needed to bring about this miracle of fruitfulness in my life. You have said I can be so much more. Yes, let it be so."

But the bride isn't merely looking for fruitfulness in her life for her own satisfaction. She seeks it with a purpose. "Let my beloved come to his garden and eat its pleasant fruits." She says, "Yes, Lord!" - even, "More, Lord!" - that He might find joy in her.

The bridegroom answers, "I have come to my garden, my sister, my spouse; I have gathered my myrrh with my spice; I have eaten my honeycomb with my honey; I have drunk my wine with my milk" (Song 5:1).

While the bride is seeking the future fulfillment of all that her bridegroom has spoken regarding her, the bridegroom assures her he is pleased with her as she is now. He says, "I have come . . . I have gathered . . . I have eaten . . . I have drunk."

There remains hope and a promise for her future, but the present is sweet. The fellowship they share is precious and satisfying. The bridegroom loves his bride as she is. She doesn't have to wait to give him pleasure. She doesn't have to grow to give him joy. She doesn't have to change to be loved.

The final words of this passage are a blessing upon the communion of the bride and bridegroom. I take it as the voice of the Father who says, "Eat, O friends! Drink, yes, drink deeply, O beloved ones!" (Song 5:1).

The words, "Eat, O friends! Drink, yes drink deeply, O beloved ones!" have the same feel to me as the Genesis blessing on Adam and Eve. Father God is intentional in His blessing on the union of the bride and bridegroom. Their oneness is His joy. They have come together in communion of soul, eating and drinking deeply in their love, and the blessing of the Father is over it all, even as it has been from the beginning.

As I pondered these things, I felt a whisper in my heart. "Stay a little while with me," I heard the Lord entreat me. "Stay and listen. Let your mind be still of its constant mechanisms. Let your soul be calm. Quiet the voices that disturb your peace. Please, just stay a little while with me. Stay until your nearness satisfies me, your trust blesses me, and your love fills my cup to overflowing. Stay and give your love to me. This is my heart's desire."

"Drink deeply, my Beloved."

Yes, Lord. I will.

PART IV

"I sleep, but my heart is awake;
It is the voice of my beloved!
He knocks, saying,
"Open for me, my sister, my love, my dove, my perfect one;
For my head is covered with dew,
My locks with the drops of the night."

I have taken off my robe;
How can I put it on again?
I have washed my feet;
How can I defile them?
My beloved put his hand
By the latch of the door,
And my heart yearned for him.
I arose to open for my beloved,
And my hands dripped with myrrh,
My fingers with liquid myrrh
On the handles of the lock.
I opened for my beloved,

But my beloved had turned away and was gone.
My heart leaped up when he spoke.
I sought him, but I could not find him;
I called him, but he gave me no answer.
The watchmen who went about the city found me.
They struck me, they wounded me;
The keepers of the walls
Took my veil away from me.

I charge you, O daughters of Jerusalem,
If you find my beloved,
That you tell him I am lovesick!

What is your beloved
More than another beloved,
O fairest among women?
What is your beloved
More than another beloved,
That you so charge us?
My beloved is white and ruddy,
Chief among ten thousand.
His head is like the finest gold;
His locks are wavy,
And black as a raven.
His eyes are like doves
By the river of waters,
Washed with milk,
And fitly set.
His cheeks are like a bed of spices,
Banks of scented herbs.
His lips are lilies,
Dripping liquid myrrh.
His hands are rods of gold
Set with beryl.
His body is carved ivory

Inlaid with sapphires.
His legs are pillars of marble
Set on bases of fine gold.
His countenance is like Lebanon,
Excellent as the cedars.

His mouth is sweet,
Yes, he is altogether lovely.
This is my beloved,
And this is my friend,
O daughters of Jerusalem!

Where has your beloved gone,
O fairest among women?
Where has your beloved turned aside,
That we may seek him with you?

My beloved has gone to his garden,
To the beds of spices,
To feed his flock in the gardens,
And to gather lilies.
I am my beloved's,
And my beloved is mine.
He feeds his flock among the lilies.

O my love, you are as beautiful as Tirzah,
Lovely as Jerusalem,
Awesome as an army with banners!
Turn your eyes away from me,
For they have overcome me.
Your hair is like a flock of goats
Going down from Gilead.
Your teeth are like a flock of sheep
Which have come up from the washing;
Every one bears twins,

And none is barren among them.
Like a piece of pomegranate
Are your temples behind your veil.

There are sixty queens
And eighty concubines,
And virgins without number.
My dove, my perfect one
Is the only one,
The only one of her mother,
The favorite of the one who bore her.
The daughters saw her
And called her blessed,
The queens and the concubines,
And they praised her.
Who is she who looks forth as the morning,
Fair as the moon,
Clear as the sun,
Awesome as an army with banners?

OPEN FOR ME

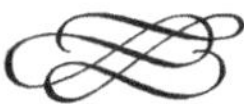

At the conclusion of the previous section, the bride was in her bridegroom's arms, surrounded by the assurance of his love for her. His declaration of love, his unwavering commitment to her, has become her greatest treasure. This is the love she has always wished for; this sense of belonging, of being known, of being loved while fully understood. This is something she will do anything to preserve. This love is too precious to lose. Unconsciously, the bride now does what most of us would do. She sets herself to keep the treasure she cannot bear to lose.

The bride says, "I sleep, but my heart is awake; it is the voice of my beloved! He knocks, saying, 'Open for me, my sister, my love, my dove, my perfect one; for my head is covered with dew, my locks with the drops of the night.' I have taken off my robe; how can I put it on again? I have washed my feet; how can I defile them? My beloved put his hand by the latch and my heart yearned for him. I arose to open for my beloved, and my hands dripped with myrrh, my fingers with liquid myrrh on the handles of the lock" (Song 5:2-5).

For years there has been a sign in a shop window in my town which reads, "God loves us just the way we are, but He loves us too much to leave us that way."

This saying may catch our attention, but most of us don't really believe it. We are glad to think God loves us as we are, and agree He wants to change us. (I have yet to meet a man or a woman who feels they have arrived at perfection in God's sight.) The problem is most of us believe it is up to us to change ourselves. Somehow, we think once God forgives our sins and cleans up our lives, it is then up to us to stay clean and never let Him down. Most of us do what the bride has done in the opening of this passage. We protect our personal righteousness for the sake of our God.

Protecting personal righteousness is not a big issue for a baby Christian. Most who are new to faith acknowledge their helplessness to walk in the goodness of God. They are amazed and thrilled at God's forgiveness, and at the kindness which for the first time in their lives gives them the freedom to experience goodness in their hearts. But for those who have walked with the Lord for a while, the situation the bride now faces becomes a very real issue.

The odd thing is, as soon as we see ourselves continually falling short of God's goodness, we tend to redouble our efforts to be good. We try to separate ourselves from what we see as the evil nature within us. We think we can maintain goodness if we only try harder. Unconsciously, we subscribe to the twelve-steps-to-holiness program. We see our Sunday morning meetings and our weekly Bible studies as our support groups. But it is so hard, and there are holes in our hearts that all the trying cannot fill.

As a result, one of two things occur. We fail in our "holiness program" and are too ashamed to admit to the secret vises that keep us bound, or we become so rigid in our way of living we epitomize a "good Christian" on the outside, while we are dry and empty on the inside. People look to us as the standard and come to us for counsel. We quote the Scriptures and pray with them, despite the void within ourselves; all the while we are wondering how long we can maintain the charade.

Yet, through all of this, we still believe the gospel is true. There is no other answer to the need of mankind to experience forgiveness for sin. In the midst of our emptiness, we remember what we once had: the joy, the sense of freedom, the peace. We think, *If only we could overcome the evil desires in our hearts, if only we could stir ourselves to believe a little more, then everything would be alright.* We try so hard to do everything right, but find these behaviors do not produce holiness in us. When we attempt to substitute our efforts toward goodness for our connection to Jesus, we inevitably find ourselves in the state in which the bride now finds herself.

We are trapped, and who can save us? All our efforts to please God have brought us to a standstill. We thought we could be clean if we only remembered, if we only maintained what was once so life-giving to us. But it has become hard to hear the Voice that once sounded so joyously in our hearts. The Voice is distant now, muffled, if it sounds at all. We remember perhaps there was much in the Christian life in which we once took pleasure. The word of God was like a garden in springtime bursting with life, begging for discovery. But now we just go through the motions because that is what we are supposed to do. If we remember what we felt at first, it seems like a distant dream.

In this passage the bride begins, "I sleep, but my heart is awake; it is the voice of my beloved! He knocks, saying, 'Open for me . . .'"

"I sleep, but my heart is awake." The sleep mentioned here is not a restful repose at the end of the day; it is a word which means slack or languid. It describes a dulling of the senses, a loss of awareness. Life has crowded in on her, distancing her from her relationship with her beloved. Her senses are dulled, yet her heart hears a voice. A familiar, beloved voice calls to her.

The bridegroom knocks, saying, "Open for me." How very like the

Lord this is. He sees the condition his bride is in, and he doesn't say, "Fix yourself." He says instead, "Let me in."

This calls to mind another time when the Lord knocks at the heart of His bride, in Revelation 3, at the close of the letter to the church of Laodicea. He has described the condition of her heart. She looks good on the outside, but on the inside, there is no fire, no passion, just a languor; an indifference to the things which stir His heart. He says she doesn't know this about herself, but it is a deadly condition. There is a warning and an entreaty to receive what He offers to correct her condition and then He says, "Behold, I stand at the door and knock. If anyone hears My voice and opens the door, I will come in to him and dine with him, and he with Me" (Revelation 3:20, NKJV).

"Let Me in that I may dine with you." Not let me in that I may punish you, condemn you, shame you. He says, "Let me in. I want to have fellowship with you. I want to share my heart with you. I want you to share your heart with me. Let me in. I want to be your friend."

"Open for me" is very like "Let him kiss me." We never get beyond our need of Him. We never arrive at a place where our own strength or goodness is sufficient to carry us. Every day, from the beginning to the end of our lives, we need Him. He understands this. The struggle to accept it is within ourselves.

MY SISTER

"My sister, my love, my dove, my perfect one . . ." (Song 5:2).

The bridegroom says, "Open for me, my sister." The identification indicated by this address is important for us to recognize. It is actually a door for us into the Lord's heart. When the bridegroom calls the bride "my sister," he is saying, "I am like you. I understand you." He has joined her in the elemental aspects of her being. He has embraced in his own person the things that identify her.

I once watched a video of a master potter working clay on a wheel. The clay was not clean. It was muddy and wet and very messy. The lump of clay was not attractive to me. If I had been the one to work with it, I would have stood back and touched it carefully with only my hands. But the potter took hold of it eagerly. He used his hands, his arms, even his shoulders to shape and form the clay into the pot he was designing. In fact, as he molded and shaped and expertly formed the clay, I was fascinated by the way he put his whole body into his work, so he appeared to be actually embracing that soggy, messy lump of clay.

By the time he was finished, clay was matted in his hair. Clay covered his face. It was in his mouth and ears. There was not more than an inch or two of his clothing that remained clay free. He looked like a clay man. He seemed to be made of the same material that sat in splendor on his wheel; and he was alight with joy. I have never seen anyone so oblivious to being covered in dirt. He truly seemed to love the clay and to glory in his involvement with it.

As I watched that potter, I thought about Jesus. He put on flesh and became a man. He felt everything we feel. He was cold. He was hot. He got sunburned and tired. He stubbed His toes. He mashed his fingers. He tasted fresh grapes from the vine and savory meat from the spit.

He watched the sea gulls circle over the sea and listened to the doves cooing for their mates in the trees. He breathed in the crisp morning air and saw the sun come up over the mountains as the sky turned from purple, to pink, to blue. He rejoiced in the world we enjoy. But most of all, He loved the people in His life.

He loved the people. He had loved them always, but now for the first time, He was able to embrace them, to put His arms around them, to hold their hands and be involved in their lives. He was not standing at a safe distance, gingerly touching messy mankind with pristine fingertips. He had dived headfirst into the flesh we wear. He took the clay that houses our souls and formed a clay house for His divine nature. He became a man, and He called Himself our brother.

The bridegroom says, "Open for me, my sister." This is a beginning point for her, if she can believe it. If the bride can accept her bridegroom is her brother; that he identifies with her in the weaknesses and struggles she faces, she will be better able to trust him to have real answers for her needs.

How is it possible for us to trust someone with the deepest needs in our hearts if we do not believe they have ever felt those needs for themselves? I believe the most basic emotional need of mankind is to be loved. To feel truly loved, we must feel we are truly understood. When we know a person has shared our circumstances and felt our pain, we are more likely to receive his compassion and to grasp his hand when he extends it to lead us out of the quagmire of pain and confusion in our lives. Identification is key to trust.

I have long accepted I am clay; with that there has been an unfolding understanding that in this human frailty, I am loved. The amazement I have felt over the love poured out on me, and the struggle I have had to be still and receive love in the midst of a deep awareness of my human state, has been much of the focus of my devotion times. But God doesn't stop with merely giving us His love.

Like finding a door in a solid wall, one day the Lord gave me a new understanding of the four glories of man represented in wood, silver, gold, and purple – the materials used in the palanquin. Remember, wood shows the glory of the created, silver the glory of the redeemed, gold speaks of the glory of the sanctified, and purple the glory of the glorified.

I had always seen myself as the wood, remaining wood despite His ornamentation, until I began to understand the Lord wants me to recognize His transforming power in my life.

The Lord wants us to take hold of this truth: we are not merely wood covered in silver by His kindness, but we are silver in Him. We are gold. We are even purple.

God is not only covering us. He is transforming us by the power of the cross. We are not ornamented wood destined to spend our lives hiding the stigma of our sins beneath the covering of Jesus' sacrifice. We carry, instead, the likeness of the one who has given us His nature.

Now we are in Him and the glory of the created has become the beauty of Eden. It is the wonder of being called "sister" by the Man who laid aside His divinity to wear a house of flesh. The glory of the created is a glory because the Creator takes delight in who we are. We are new in Him. We are alright. We are like the sparkling water in the sunshine. We are clay. We are man, and God said, "It is good" (Genesis 1:31).

The second name the bridegroom calls the bride is "my love" (Song 5:2). If calling the bride "my sister" expresses the bridegroom's identification with his bride, calling her "my love" expresses his commitment to her. This is the love that will not let go. This love, once given, is never taken back. This love is steady and unyielding. It never wavers. It does not deter from its purpose. This love is wholly committed to doing all that is best for the loved one.

There is a phrase in Paul's letter to the Corinthians which is translated, "the love of Christ constrains us" (2 Corinthians 5:14, DARBY). He is talking about the passion in his heart to give away what God has given him, but I love the word "constrain." It is a word which means to compel, but the root means "to hold together" or "to grip tightly." It has the sense of being held fast. There is no escape.

I cannot tell you how many times I have depended on His promise to hold me no matter what. When I have felt totally undeserving of His love, when I have been most aware of how very far away my heart was from His, when I have turned away from Him in the certainty there was no reason for Him to love me, I have heard Him whisper, "I've got you, baby."

This is a phrase no other person has ever spoken to me. It does not come from my memory or imagination. But it floats up from the innermost parts of my being at times when I am sad, discouraged, or afraid. I am held in the grip of Love and He will not let me go.

The second glory of man – silver - is the glory of the redeemed. "My love" is the name the bridegroom uses to express this condition to his bride. She isn't just someone toward whom he feels affection. She is held in the grip of his love, and Love has determined to do all that is needed to give her life.

How high, how wide, how deep is the love of God? ". . . neither death nor life, nor angels nor principalities nor powers, nor things present nor things to come, nor height nor depth, nor any other created thing, shall be able to separate us from the love of God which is in Christ Jesus our Lord" (Romans 8:38-39, NKJV).

Many have written of the lengths to which God went to redeem our lives from destruction. From the simple question put to Jesus, "How much do you love me?" and His answer, "I love you this much," as He stretched out His arms and He died, we have been shown the cost. But do we also see the prize?

Are we guilty criminals still? Or are we a treasure worth dying for, a bride? What is God seeking from us but that we would allow His inescapable love to permeate our hearts? That what we perceive as waste would be given value in our sight? That we would look again at the dross of our lives and see that love has worked a transformation? We are precious. We are cherished. No longer ashamed, we are worthy. We are silver; redeemed. "Open for me, my love."

MY DOVE

"Open for me . . . my dove" (Song 5:2).

I stood in the church as the musicians played. I sang the words and tried to turn my thoughts toward the Lord, but other thoughts kept getting in the way, ugly thoughts. I realized I was more focused on myself than on God, and no matter how much I tried to turn my thoughts and fix my heart, I couldn't do it.

Frustrated and sad, I said, "God, what are you going to do about me?" Immediately, I felt Him smile. It was as if He was waiting for me to ask for His help. Then I saw tiny gold flakes falling like a fine snow until I was covered head to toe. By this He made me understand that what He saw when I worshiped was the beauty of His holiness upon me.

So I stood in His freedom and worshiped with all of the love in my heart. Later, a woman nearby said she had been watching as I worshiped. She told me it was so sweet that it helped her to overcome her struggles and enter into His presence, too.

The dove speaks of the presence of the Holy Spirit. It is the Holy Spirit who sanctifies. When He is present, holiness happens. The Holy Spirit comes and fills the bride, surrounding her in the purity and goodness of God.

Through the embrace of the Holy Spirit, we are lifted into the presence of our Father. The Holy Spirit swallows up all the distance between us and causes the clamoring voices to fade. He leads us into the freedom that is found in the immediacy of our Father's love.

"My dove . . ." We are gold. We are holy.

MY PERFECT ONE

"My perfect one . . ." (Song 5:2).

As difficult as it is for us to believe and accept the names sister, love, and dove, I think "my perfect one" may be the hardest. Since we live inside of ourselves, we know it's impossible to think of ourselves as perfect.

If you are like me, perfect means good and upright in every way. Perfect is never making a mistake, never missing an opportunity to show love; it is never becoming angry, or frustrated, or discouraged. Perfect is doing everything with excellence. Perfect is beyond me. I know it.

So when I hear the words, "my perfect one," without further thought, I push them away as something that cannot apply to me. But I must ask, has Jesus ever said anything that is not true? Can God lie? If I believe the answer is "no," then I need to find out how to believe that "my perfect one" means me.

In the Old Testament the Hebrew word for perfect is "Tam." It contains the meanings: complete, undefiled, and coupled together (as in two becoming one). The Greek word in the New Testament for perfect is similar. "Teleios" means: that which has reached an end, finished, complete. It speaks of soundness, wholeness, and maturity.

As I looked at these words and prayed over the Scripture's use of "perfect" in the Old and New Testaments, I began to wonder – when God says "perfect one" what if He isn't referring to attitudes or behaviors on our part? What if He is speaking of something much more personal to Himself? What if He is inviting us to come into a place within Himself that will fill and complete everything within us that is lacking?

I think it would help to remember the context. The bridegroom says, "Open for me my sister, my love, my dove, my perfect one." When Jesus dove into our humanity and became our brother, He came and got us. He took hold of us in love and poured out His goodness on us. Now He offers us a place in Himself that leads us into the fullness of our Father's kind intentions toward us.

One of the sweetest passages that speaks of being made perfect is found in John's gospel. Jesus prayed, " . . . [F]or those who will believe in Me . . . that they all may be one, as You, Father, are in Me, and I in You; that they also may be one in Us . . . and the glory which You gave Me I have given them, that they may be one just as We are one: I in them, and You in Me; that they may be made perfect in one" (John 17:20-23, NKJV).

"I in them and You in Me . . . made perfect in one." I don't see anything about excellence in attitude or behavior in this. To Jesus, being perfect is about relationship - our oneness with Himself and Father. So, I must now ask, what hinders me from this oneness? What idea of perfection is holding me back from the fullness that is in God's heart for me?

Do I insist my frailty is sufficient to keep me from oneness with Him? My humanness? My sinfulness? Jesus shed His blood for my sin, and Jesus calls me "sister." There is no barrier there. He shares my human state.

Do I maintain that I am too capricious? Too unpredictable? Too fickle? My history shows I cannot trust that I will be faithful when life is hard. But Jesus called me His "love." He has taken hold of me with a grip that will never lose its hold. I am safe in His arms.

Do I insist upon attaining a level of personal goodness before I will give God the freedom to pour out His goodness on me? Jesus said we must come as little children, turning our hearts toward our Father in trust and dependence, in order to enter the kingdom. We cannot make ourselves good enough to deserve oneness with God. We can only receive the goodness He gives so willingly to those who turn toward Him in simple trust.

What hinders me from oneness with God? Is it that I must do certain acts of kindness? Reach a level of generosity in what I possess? Do I need to pray more, read the Bible more? Do I make it about what I do or fail to do? Jesus doesn't. He looks at a heart that wants Him, a face turned toward Him with longing, and He says, "Mine." He draws us into His heart, and declares we are complete because of His fullness. He gives Himself to us and then He teaches us how to give ourselves to Him.

"Open for me, my sister, my love, my dove, my perfect one" has become a constant refrain in my spirit. With every failure, every time I struggle to bring my heart into agreement with His, every time I feel weak or insignificant, I hear Him whisper, "Open for me. Let me have access to this place in your heart. I want to fill you, empower you, and make you free."

DEW AND DROPS

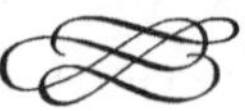

"My head is covered with dew,
my locks with the drops of the night" (Song 5:2).

At first glance these two metaphors seem to be poetic redundancy, but I have come to see them as companions revealing the mind of God toward the bride.

His head refers to His power and authority. The dew speaks of blessing, the promise of a new day. When the bridegroom says, "my head is covered with dew," it is like the Lord saying, "Love hopes all things." The one who loves us sees what He is capable of doing. His thoughts toward us are filled with promise and blessing.

The bridegroom's locks are a reference to his hair, and by extension Jesus' human state. Jesus was covered with "drops of the night" the night He prayed in Gethsemane. The pain and fear and grief of this world were pressed upon Him as He prayed for strength to carry it to the cross. There is not one desperate thought, not one sorrow or pain, not one dark thing in the human experience that escaped Him that night. Not only was He touched by it all, He took it. He carried it away and left it in the grave.

So when the bridegroom came to the bride seeking entrance, he offered her both the hope of the blessing contained in the morning dew, and the declaration that all of her darkness had been laid upon him. He says, "Open for me, my sister, my love, my dove, my perfect one; for my head is covered with dew, my locks with the drops of the night."

"Let me in, my darling. There is nothing to hinder our oneness. Do not keep me outside. I have taken you into my heart. Will you now also take me into yours?"

I HAVE WASHED

$\mathcal{S}$adly, the bride responds, "I have taken off my robe; how can I put it on again? I have washed my feet; how can I defile them?" (Song 5:3). She says, "I have laid aside my clothes. I don't want to dress again. I have made myself clean. I don't want to wash again." So she leaves him standing at the door, more mindful of her own state than of his request for entrance.

How tidy is your world? How orderly is your involvement with God? Have you taken off your robe; laid aside your worldly life? Have you bathed your feet – cleaned up your walk?

How genuine is your love for God? Would you mind very much if He requested you join Him in a situation which would require a change in your concept of what it is to do things "decently and in order?" Would you agree to allow Him in when what He brings with Him challenges your comfortable world?

He said, "My head is covered with dew, my locks with the drops of the night." He was outside, while she had grown comfortable in her place. This is surely a challenge to the bride's orderly life.

I will never forget when God turned my religious world upside down. I had been hearing of strange things God was doing among Christians in other places. Even members of my own family had been touched by these unusual things. I was certain it couldn't be from God and had even advised a close friend to be cautious about these things, saying, "God is a gentleman and does things decently and in order." You see, my god was starched and clean, with manicured nails and every hair in place.

I didn't know this about myself. I believed I was compassionate and caring toward others. I sang on the worship team and lifted my hands. I prayed aloud and gave thanks to God. But in many ways my world was as orderly and controlled as the bride's in this passage.

When news of the powerful things God was doing began to touch people close to me, I asked the Lord if this was from Him and if He wanted me to pursue Him in it. In answer He took me to 2 Samuel 6, where the Ark of the Covenant was being brought into Jerusalem.

The presence of God was being restored to the people and King David rejoiced. In his excitement, David laid aside his robes and danced for joy with all his might as he led the procession with the ark into the city. But there was one who watched the proceedings with displeasure, Michal, the daughter of Saul.

She criticized David for his "unseemly display," but David answered her rebuke by saying in effect, "I did not do this for your benefit, nor for anyone else's either. I danced to give pleasure to God."

When I read this passage, I felt the Lord ask me, "Will you give me your dignity and your reputation? Will you lay them aside as David did with his kingly robes? Will you let me redefine your concept of order? Will you dance with me?"

I didn't answer immediately. I knew this was going to cost me. I knew what the Lord was asking would bring unpleasant attention to my life. I would be criticized and mocked. I didn't want to be uncomfortable. I was happy with my orderly church life. I was happy—except for the lack of the presence and power of God.

LIQUID MYRRH

"My beloved put his hand by the latch of the door, and my heart
yearned for him. I arose to open for my beloved. And my hands
dripped with myrrh, my fingers with liquid myrrh, on the handles
of the lock. I opened for my beloved, but my beloved had
turned away and was gone" (Song 5:4-6).

Not willing to leave without trying again to gain entrance,
the bridegroom tries to open the door. Finally, the bride's
heart is moved as her focus shifts from her own state to his. But she is
slow in coming, preoccupied with the liquid myrrh that drips from
her fingers. When she at last opens the door for him, he has gone
away.

"My hands dripped with myrrh, my fingers with liquid myrrh." Myrrh
on the hands and dripping from the fingers, pictures the soul-satis-
fying activities with which the bride busies herself. These are not bad
things, except that they have preempted her relationship with her

bridegroom. She has substituted busyness on behalf of others for intimacy with him. Her preoccupation with these things has her slow in coming to the door.

This is a common situation among sincere believers. There is a short step from having a daily quiet time of reading the Bible while listening to the Lord to studying for the sake of knowledge. Studying is good, but it cannot take the place of listening quietly to the Lord. What we do to serve others and better ourselves can become a thief of intimacy through substitution.

The loss of intimacy through good activities is usually gradual and subtle. Like the sleep of the bride, we do not even recognize the dulling of our senses. We are busy with helping and serving other people, often too busy to notice the loss and the distance from the Lord. Or if we do notice, we may feel distress, but our activities require so much of us we don't take the time to discover the source of our discomfort and correct it. We are involved in church. We are praying and studying the Bible. We are helping people. What could be the problem in that?

Jesus said, "I know your works, your labor, your patience, and that you cannot bear those who are evil . . . you have persevered and have patience and have labored for My name's sake and have not become weary. Nevertheless, I have this against you, that you have left your first love. Remember therefore from where you have fallen; repent and do the first works, or else I will come to you quickly and remove your lampstand from its place – unless you repent" (Revelation 2:2-5, NKJV).

The message is clear. Loss of intimacy with God through busyness and good works is serious; serious enough to lose our light. This may be a common thing, and we may comfort ourselves that it's what we see modeled by others, even by leadership in the church; but it is not something to ignore or accept. Jesus called it a fallen state.

He said to correct it we must intentionally turn and do the first works. What are the first works? Loving Jesus, listening for His voice, taking time to be in His presence just for the joy of knowing Him. When we first began to know the Lord, every one of us had an honest, unsophisticated approach to God. It is this that we dare not lose.

SEARCHING IN THE NIGHT

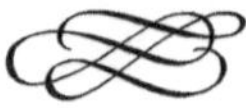

"I opened for my beloved, but my beloved had turned away
and was gone. My heart leaped up when he spoke.
I sought him, but I could not find him; I called him,
but he gave me no answer" (Song 5:6).

This is the second time the bride's hesitation over the bridegroom's invitation has her searching the city for him at night. When she opened the door, the bridegroom had gone away. She went in search of him but did not find him. She called, but he did not answer.

"The watchmen who went about the city found me.
They struck me, they wounded me; the keepers
of the walls took my veil away from me" (Song 5:7).

Watchmen are those who keep watch over the city for purposes of its well-being. When they saw the bride they struck her, wounded her, and took her veil away. Proverbs 27:5-6 (NKJV) says, "Open rebuke is better Than love carefully concealed. Faithful are the wounds of a friend . . ."

As strange as it may seem, I believe the violence done to the bride at this time is a kindness. It is sometimes needful to have someone care enough to rebuke us in order to jolt us into change. The keepers of the walls took her veil away. She wore the veil for the anonymity it provided; having it removed is reminiscent of the blind man who cried out to Jesus for mercy. He cast his beggar's cloak beside the road, essentially leaving the security of his former life in his search for something more (Mark 10:46-52).

In her search for her bridegroom, the bride loses her self-protective covering. Her restraints for appearance' sake are cast aside. Suddenly the most important thing to her has become that she find her bridegroom.

At last, the bride has come into agreement with the entreaty of the bridegroom. He said, "Open for me." It was not merely a request to let him into the house. He wanted into her life; into her heart in the places she had withheld from him. The titles he gave her (sister, love, dove, perfect one) were more than terms of endearment. They were promises of his faithfulness operating in her life.

When she eventually overcame her hesitation and opened the door, he was gone. This was not a punishment, nor a situation of "had your chance, missed it." The bridegroom was leading her out. She still had some things to fully release. It was necessary for her to pursue him in order for those changes in her to have their full effect.

She likely struggled with the loss of her veil. Losing our shields is never comfortable. But she wouldn't allow herself to be distracted from her purpose by her discomfort. The overriding emotion had become the necessity of finding her bridegroom. Instead of hiding inside a house or beneath a veil, she went into the streets and begged others to help in her search.

Making this move toward intimacy will take us into the deep. When we become more concerned about being with Jesus – whatever that requires – than about what people think of us, we have laid aside our veils. Wherever we are, whomever we're with, we are living our lives in transparency as the beloved of the Lord, and our conversation and behavior reflect it without any degree of hesitation or embarrassment. This is searching for Him in the city. This is unashamedly asking others if they have seen our Beloved One.

With the loss of her veil, the bride has become transparent and humble. She is no longer seeking the safe and tidy existence which once mattered so much to her. She cares only about finding the one who makes her life complete.

She begs the daughters of Jerusalem, "If you find my beloved, tell him I am lovesick!" (Song 5:8). Or in other words, "Tell him I am lost and empty without him." She has given up her conditions for fellowship with him that had acted as her shields. She has become so desperate she willingly does whatever is required just so she can hear his voice again.

The daughters of Jerusalem ask why they should be stirred to help her look for him. "What is your beloved more than another beloved, O fairest among women? What is your beloved more than another beloved, that you so charge us?" (Song 5:9).

The daughters of Jerusalem don't seem to recognize her; otherwise, they would certainly know for whom she is seeking. The king is a well-known person and easily identified. But they ask the bride what is so special about her beloved that they should even notice him.

What is my beloved more than any other?

I can feel the bride drawing together all the love and admiration in her heart. I can see her trying to find the words to describe this person who has so transformed her life. Is he more than any other?

She pauses, closes her eyes, and breathes in the memory of his beauty. When she speaks, it is with a new reverence. She does not speak of him in reference to herself. She does not give his name or title. She does not describe his wealth or power. She does not mention the praise of his friends or the fear of his enemies. She can think only of his person. This is her answer to them.

"My beloved is white and ruddy, chief among ten thousand. His head is like the finest gold; his locks are wavy, and black as a raven. His eyes are like doves by the rivers of waters, washed with milk, and fitly set. His cheeks are like a bed of spices, banks of scented herbs. His lips are lilies, dripping liquid myrrh. His hands are rods of gold set with beryl. His body is carved ivory inlaid with sapphires. His legs are pillars of marble set on bases of fine gold. His countenance is like Lebanon, excellent as the cedars. His mouth is most sweet, yes, he is altogether lovely. This is my beloved, and this is my friend, O daughters of Jerusalem!" (Song 5:10-15).

WHITE AND RUDDY

The account of creation begins, "God said, 'Let there be light'" (Genesis 1:3). The description of the bridegroom begins, "My beloved is white" (Song 5:10).

While translated "white," this word means "bright or dazzling," filled with light. The light that shines from him is so great it dazzles, like the light of the sun compared to the stars. He is, in fact, the source of light.

Let us pause for a moment and consider this thought. Our Bridegroom is light. In a world of uncertainty, where the very ground beneath our feet is unstable; the oceans are swaying and washing over the shores with the slipping of fissures on the ocean floor. Things we have always understood to be permanent have lost their comforting strength in our minds. Yet our Bridegroom is light. Light: the foundation for all matter.

Everything of creation was created by light. Light-waves, soundwaves, and matter share a common source: the elemental things of atoms, photons, neutrons, and electrons. In the tangible world, light pulses, explodes, heats, burns, cooks, warms, and gives sight. In the intangible world, light lifts, encourages, enriches, enlivens, refreshes, calms, and imparts understanding and wisdom.

In John 1:4-5 we read of Jesus, "In Him was life, and the life was the light of men. And the light shines in the darkness, and the darkness did not comprehend (control, or overpower) it."

Jesus said, ". . . I am the light of the world. He who follows Me shall not walk in darkness, but have the light of life" (John 8:12, NKJV).

When we approach our Bridegroom through this doorway, we find in Him the light that overcomes all darkness. He is the very light that created the world.

"My beloved is white and ruddy." The bride states her bridegroom is both white and ruddy. If this description were in reference to his complexion, it would seem contradictory. Ruddy in the traditional sense refers to having a healthy complexion or having reddish colored hair. But as the word for white references much more than the color of the bridegroom's skin, the word for ruddy goes far beyond physical appearance.

The word translated "ruddy" is "adom." It shares its root with "adam," the word for mankind. The bride is not merely stating her bridegroom is in excellent health, but he is a man, a human being.

Jesus loved to call Himself "the Son of Man." In fact, throughout the gospels I found eighty references of Jesus speaking of Himself with this title. In contrast, He called Himself the Son of God in only five references. (There are more recorded incidences in the Gospels of the devil calling Jesus by the title "Son of God" than of Jesus doing so.)

Jesus is the living word. He was the sound of Father's voice at creation. When the waters gathered and dry land appeared, He was there. When the earth brought forth trees bearing seeds after their kind, He participated. He was with His Father when He formed clay into the shape of a man and breathed life into his being. And yet He delights to call Himself the Son of Man. Why? What is there about being the Son of Man that pleases Him to that degree? I am still pondering this one. I have found a door into the heart of God. I believe it will take eternity to explore.

As the first word, "white," declares His divinity, so the second word, "ruddy," declares His humanity. Our Bridegroom is eternally, inseparably both God and man.

POWERFUL AND GOOD

*H*e is "chief among ten thousand" (Song 5:10) is similar to our saying, "one in a million." Ten thousand is an idiom in Hebrew which represents an undefined multitude. It is often translated as "myriads." The bridegroom is unlike any other man among men. He is in a class above all others.

This address also describes him as the leader, the head over multitudes. The covenant name of God most often used in the Old Testament is YHWH Tseboath, translated "the Lord of Hosts." The bride could as easily have said her bridegroom is the lord of hosts.

I have felt the fierceness of God's love as I prayed for innocents whose lives were damaged by evil. It felt like the roar of a lion. It was not an anguished cry, but a militant, powerful roar of redemption and vindication. Even the sound the Holy Spirit brought through me at those times came forth like a roar. It is not a sound I am able to produce on my own. When the sound arose through my being, I was very aware that God was pledging Himself to redeem everything that had been stolen, and to vindicate every wrong on behalf of His beloved child. I believe I was feeling the heartbeat of the Lord of Hosts, the Lion of the Tribe of Judah, He who is chief among ten thousand.

"His head is like the finest gold" (Song 5:11). No flaws. No impurities. He is honestly who he is. He is truly good. His thoughts are golden. His will is good. He does not think as others, with selfishness and darkness shadowing his desires. He does not dominate and control those in his care. His head is gold. He leads with goodness, with fairness, and with integrity.

The bride describes the bridegroom's head, hands, and feet as made of gold. The consecration of Aaron as high priest took place through applying the blood of the burnt offering to his right ear, the thumb of his right hand, and the large toe of his right foot. That the bridegroom's head, hands, and feet are gold points to his position as our perfect High Priest. The sanctification that readied Aaron for his office as priest before God is clearly shown in the person of our Bridegroom.

Gold speaks of holiness, of being one with God. The references to golden head, hands, and feet indicates our Bridegroom is one with God in all He thinks and does, and in every place His feet carry Him.

Jesus said, "I can of Myself do nothing" (John 5:30, NKJV), and, "I and *My* Father are One" (John 10:30, NKJV). Every merciful act of Jesus originated in the heart of His Father.

"His locks are wavy and black as a raven" (Song 5:11). His hair is thick and dark and curly. It is touchable, human. His head is gold, but His hair is wavy and thick. Once again, we see in our bridegroom a person who is both God and man. He is good, yet He is warm, approachable, real.

GENTLE AND TRUE

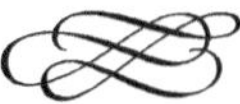

"His eyes are like doves by the rivers of waters,
washed with milk and fitly set" (Song 5:12).

The bridegroom is strong and regal and handsome, a leader among men and a tower of strength to the bride. But he is not harsh or distant.

Doves are small silvery birds which make a gentle cooing sound. Their feathers, although grey, have an iridescence which glistens emerald and sapphire in the sunshine. Doves embody gentleness, kindness, and peace. The image of the bridegroom's eyes like doves beside a river describes the depths and mysteries; the wisdom and understanding found in his eyes. When we stand on the bank of a river, we do not see where it comes from or where it is going. Its birthplace is a mystery, and the secrets it carries as it journeys to the sea are fathomless.

I can hear the bride say these words with a wistful sigh of longing as she envisions the face of her bridegroom, "His eyes are like doves by the rivers of waters." The tenderness he feels toward her is revealed in his eyes. He sees her, truly sees her, as no other has ever done.

Our bridegroom is the one "who is, and was, and is to come" (Revelation 1:8, NIV). In the same way, the river is and was and goes on from here. The river carries secrets and mysteries within it, just as His eyes contain the wisdom of the Ancient of Days.

"Washed with milk and fitly set" speaks of the beauty of his eyes, but also of the clarity found within them. He can neither be deceived, nor is he false toward others. When the bride thinks of his eyes, she remembers the gentle embrace of his soul wrapping about her and the confidence she feels in his clear look. There are no shadows in his eyes. No uncertainties or doubts. His eyes display a quiet strength and a clear resolve. His eyes invite her to rest in the safety of his soul.

"His cheeks are like a bed of spices, banks of scented herbs" (Song 5:13). The beard on his face is fragrant with his wonderful scent. The image is of a raised bed of sweet flowers. His scent stirs within her the memory of their closeness, being held in his arms, being cherished. This is another image bringing into focus the reality of the humanity of our Bridegroom.

"His lips are lilies dripping liquid myrrh" (Song 5:13).

Lilies are a trumpet flower. During Israel's time in the wilderness trumpets were used for directing the movement of the camps. The word for "dripping" can mean to prophesy and liquid myrrh points to the powerful anointing on the words he speaks. His words not only carry the call to lead her to see what he wants for her, but they also impart the grace to enable her to enter into it.

The bride envisions the lips of her beloved as "lilies, dripping liquid myrrh." They are words filled with destiny and direction for her life. They are words which infuse her with strength and courage, enabling her to do what he is calling her to do.

RODS OF GOLD

"His hands are rods of gold set with beryl" (Song 5:14).

This image is one of the surprising passages in the Song. I thought, what very odd wording, "rods of gold," but now – well, you will see.

The word translated "rod" is "galiyl." It is the valve or hinge of a folding door. The word is used in three places in the Old Testament. In Esther 1:6 it refers to the silver rings used for the curtains in Ahasuerus' palace, but in the Song the rings are gold. There is only one other place where this word is used to describe gold rings.

In 1 Kings 6:34, "galiyl" is translated "folding" in the description of the doors leading into the sanctuary of the temple. Solomon knew exactly what he was saying when he compared the hands of the bridegroom to the golden hinges which open the doors into the holy place.

The bridegroom's hands are golden rods set with beryl. Beryl is a precious gem which has a high refractive quality. Beryl comes in many colors and is the name for the group of stones in which we find emerald, aquamarine, and chrysolite. The stones vary in color and hardness, but the crystalline structures are all hexagonal or six-sided.

"His hands are rods of gold set with beryl." What a precious picture for us. God, who created the heavens and the earth, searched for a way to bring us into relationship with Himself. As I read the accounts of the making of the tabernacle and later of the temple, I am deeply touched by the desire expressed by God to dwell among His people. Over and over, I find Him almost vibrating with excitement in the anticipation of being near His people. Now at last, He has found a meeting place where He can be with us and we can be with Him.

We will no longer be sent from His presence by the sin in our hearts. We will not have to bring sacrifices and blood offerings to atone for our unrighteousness. The door has been opened into the holiest place, never to be closed again, and we get to meet with Him there, face to face and heart to heart. Oh, the joy in the heart of God! Just see how He loves us!

The hands on which our fellowship hinges were pierced, and the holes remain in them to this very day. They are divine (gold) and yet they are covered in beryl, a six-sided crystal representing Jesus' humanity. (Adam was created on the sixth day. Six is the number for man.) Emmanuel has opened the way for God to be with us and for us to be with Him through rods of gold set with beryl.

CARVED IVORY

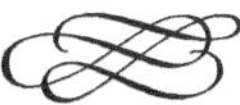

"His body is carved ivory overlaid with sapphires" (Song 5:14).

Ivory is the only exotic and valuable "jewel" that comes from mammals. Tusked animals: walruses, narwhals, but most of all, male African elephants are the source of this rare and beautiful substance. Carved ivory is highly prized for ornamentation, but it is born through suffering and is collected at the cost of the animal's life.

Although sapphires come in various colors, including pink, they are mainly found in deep blue. The Hebrew word for sapphire is "cappiyr," which comes from a root word which means: to score, inscribe, recount, show forth, write, speak, and tell.

Blue is the color of the heavens and is the color which speaks of revelation, or seeing through heaven's glass which brings clarity to a matter. "And they saw the God of Israel and there was under His feet as it were a paved work of sapphire stone, and it was like the very heavens in its clarity" (Exodus 24:10, NKJV).

Carved ivory overlaid with sapphires suggests to me the promise Jesus gave to His disciples, ". . . To you it has been given to know the mystery of the kingdom of God; but to those who are outside all things come in parables . . ." (Mark 4:11, NKJV).

A mystery is a secret which requires special revelation to be understood. The good news of our salvation brought about by the death and resurrection of our King is a mystery revealed to us by faith. To those who refuse to believe, the revelation is withheld; but to those who choose to believe, it is a truth revealed. Sapphires overlay the broken body of our Lord.

"His body is carved ivory" speaks of Jesus' suffering. "For it was fitting for Him, for whom *are* all things and by whom *are* all things, in bringing many sons to glory, to make the captain of their salvation perfect through sufferings . . . Inasmuch then as the children have partaken of flesh and blood, He Himself likewise shared in the same, that through death He might destroy him who had the power of death, that is the devil, and release those who through fear of death were all their lifetime subject to bondage" (Hebrews 2:10, 14-15, NKJV).

A long time ago I became friends with a woman who had been severely abused as a child. She came to our church about the time her memories of the abuse began to surface, and I walked alongside her for several years as she recalled many things that grieved and saddened me. One memory in particular was so horrifying that after praying with her about it, I locked it away in an effort to protect my own heart from the horror.

Years later my life was touched by another person whose situation pried the locks off that deeply buried door. I couldn't run. I couldn't hide. I needed God to help. So, I went to Jesus with this prayer, "Lord, here is my heart. All my efforts at self-protection are failing me, so I give them up. Will you take this pain and sorrow away? Will you take over the care of my heart? I'm not able to do this anymore."

I realized as I prayed that somehow, I had envisioned these terrible things as outside the redemption of God. I saw myself sitting on the far edge of hell with these two people's horrifying darkness. I didn't want to abandon them there, so I sat with them, but it seemed this darkness was too deep to be breached by light. Then I turned and saw Jesus walking toward us out of the darkness. Deep darkness was behind Him. As He came toward us, I understood that every place He had walked, He now owned. He has walked the very depths of hell, and now not one thing of human experience is outside of His ability to redeem.

Following this, the thought came to me, "His body is carved ivory overlaid with sapphires." As I continued to watch, I saw Jesus take the pain and horror of those two broken lives and lay them against the carvings of His body: the thorn and lash wounds, the nail holes, and His sword-pierced side. Before my eyes, the substance of those terrible things was absorbed by the ivory body on which they were laid. What had once appeared dark and solid and threatening now became a mere outline, transparent as air. The darkness had lost all its substance and power to hurt, but the ivory body was unchanged. The life in Jesus completely reversed the hold of darkness, but evil had absolutely no effect on Him.

> "But we see Jesus, who was made a little lower than the angels,
> for the suffering of death crowned with glory and honor,
> that He, by the grace of God might taste death for everyone"
> (Hebrews 2:9, NKJV).

Carved ivory overlaid with sapphires.

HE SHALL ESTABLISH

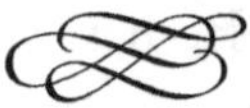

"His legs are pillars of marble set on bases of fine gold" (Song 5:15).

arble is a fine-grained stone which can be polished to a high gloss. It is a prized building material. The only other reference to marble pillars in Scripture is in the description of the king's palace in the first chapter of Esther.

The pillars in the temple Solomon built were of bronze. There is quite a detailed description of their size and ornamentation in both 1 Kings and 2 Chronicles. They stood as sentinels on either side of the entrance to the sanctuary; the pillar on the right was called Jachin and the one on the left was Boaz. Jachin means, "He shall establish." Boaz means, "In Him is strength" (1 Kings 7:21).

In Ezekiel's vision of the temple depicting our home in God and His home in us at the fullness of time, there are again two pillars at the entrance to the sanctuary. We are not told what they are made of, nor given a description of their ornamentation or size, but the location is the same as those in Solomon's temple. They stand on either side of the entrance to the holy place (Ezekiel 40:49).

Marble pillars portray permanence, stability, and authority. The marble pillars are *set* in bases of fine gold. The word for set is established. It speaks of permanence, longevity, and solidity. The marble pillars rest upon gold foundations showing us that it is God Himself who put them in place. Gold always points to holiness. Holiness belongs to God alone, so when we see something made with gold, we can see the hand of God upon it. It is by His will that we have a way of entrance into His presence.

Pillars mark the entrance to the place where God communes with His beloved. The marble pillars are not guards to prevent us from entering. They stand as an assurance of His ability to lead us in; "He shall establish" and "In Him is strength." He will help us overcome so we might sit with Him, be joined to Him, and enjoy the same oneness with God Jesus shares with His Father. His Father is our Father, too.

Psalm 89:14 (NKJV) states, "Righteousness and justice *are* the foundation of Your throne; Mercy and truth go before Your face." The twin pillars of His throne that witness to His character are righteousness and justice, while mercy and truth are the hallmarks of His countenance.

We are welcome there.

ALTOGETHER LOVELY

"His countenance is like Lebanon,
excellent as the cedars" (Song 5:15).

A countenance is more than a face, a profile, or a look. Countenance is a word which expresses a calm demeanor, an expression of approval, and a composed bearing as seen in the face.

The bride says, "His countenance is like Lebanon," comparing her bridegroom's bearing and expression to the mountain range rising above her home. Lebanon was a land of rugged ranges, snow-capped peaks, and cedar forests. Wild and wonderful, it was a place of beauty, mystery, and majesty.

When I stand on a mountain and survey the world from its height, the worries that press against me lose their strength. When I view the grandeur of a mountain, I feel my heart swell with emotion and am filled with a sense of well-being.

There is something very comforting about looking into the face of someone who loves you. They don't have to say a thing, yet you know you are accepted, and all is right with the world. The bride recalls her bridegroom's countenance and remembers that sense of well-being. Even the words, "excellent as the cedars" carry the sense of a comforting settledness, since cedars are noted for strength, beauty, and solidity.

The expression on our Bridegroom's face is open and inviting. I have seen sadness there, but never hardness or rejection. He has steadily, faithfully offered His love and acceptance through all the ups and downs of my life.

He is kind; His kindness is unshakable. He is embracing; that never changes. He is good. His goodness rises above and overshadows all of the badness of my life.

"Mercy and truth have met together" (Psalm 85:10a, NKJV). I have seen them in the countenance of my Lord.

"His mouth is most sweet" (Song 5:16) says exactly what it appears to say, with one note on the word "most." It is a word which means: something carved out, such as ore. Therefore, it carries the sense of something pure and fine, like gold. His mouth is pure, golden sweetness.

One of my favorite descriptions of what love is like comes from a four-year-old boy, named Billy, who was asked to describe love. He said, "When someone loves you, the way they say your name is different. You know that your name is safe in their mouth."

There has been one in my life who used my name in such a way as to make me want to be called by something else, and there is one whose way of saying my name leaves me in a puddle of happiness. And there is God. Nothing compares to the way He says my name.

I have heard God speak when it felt like thunder, and I have heard Him whisper tender endearments. I know I am His precious daughter, but I also know He loves each person as completely as He loves me. There is no competition for the affection of God's heart. It is freely given to each of us. The challenge before us is to learn to listen so we can hear the golden sweetness of His words to our own hearts.

"Yes, he is altogether lovely" (Song 5:16). Altogether: unitedly, withal, wholly. That's pretty much everything. Lovely: delightful, pleasant, attractive.

He is completely lovable. Not one thing about Him is scary or unworthy of our trust. You can search forever, but you will find no darkness in Him; no shadows; no twisted, selfish, bent places. He is beautiful in every way.

> "This is my beloved, and this is my friend,
> O daughters of Jerusalem" (Song 5:16).

As the bride describes her bridegroom, scales fall from her eyes. In her heart she sees him, and his character becomes clear to her. The bride's attention has been transferred from protecting her own cleanliness (I have washed my feet) to His purity (His head, hands, and feet of gold). She has lost her self-protective coverings and has been required to search for him in the city, even acknowledging her own neediness to others.

His request that she open for him has been answered, though not in the way one would think. By recounting his beauty to others, her heart has ignited with desire. Now nothing is more important to her than his presence. Nothing holds a place before him in her heart. Her love for him has become all consuming.

Suddenly the daughters of Jerusalem want to help her find him, if only to glimpse this paragon of manhood. So they ask, "Where has your beloved gone, O fairest among women? Where has your beloved turned aside, that we may seek him with you?" (Song 6:1).

Here is a paradox: the bride has asked for assistance in finding her beloved; but upon hearing the description of him the daughters of Jerusalem ask her where they should search. Suddenly, the bride realizes she knows where to look.

Recounting his beauty to the daughters of Jerusalem has turned her focus to the person of her bridegroom. It has caused the bride to turn her attention from searching for him in the city to seeing him in her heart with the surprising result that she discovers she knows where to find him.

So, she answers, "My beloved has gone to his garden, to the beds of spices, to feed his flock in the gardens, and to gather lilies. I am my beloved's, and my beloved is mine. He feeds his flock among the lilies" (Song 6:2-3).

It has all become so clear to her now, so simple. Her bridegroom is doing what he loves. He has not changed. He is not lost or hiding. She will find him again in the place she found him in the beginning. He is in the garden. She knows he loves her, and she will find him waiting for her there.

IN THE GARDEN

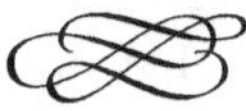

I want to weep as I conclude this section. This passage has been my meditation for several years as I have searched for the jewels within it to share with you. The phrase, "Open for me, my sister, my love, my dove, my perfect one," has become a refrain within my heart as the Lord has mined the hidden places within me and removed the veils I have used to hide and protect myself.

I am on a journey into intimacy. Jesus is leading me into oneness with the heart of God. Sometimes it has been painful, but the pain has been momentary, and the rewards are beyond description. I wish I could take your hand and lead you along this path I have walked. You would join me in wonder, and we would bow together in worship. There can be no other response but to worship; God is so amazing.

Just as the bride discovered, I have learned that all my attempts at goodness only result in separation from God. Even though my behavior may be admirable, my best efforts to do, to please, to work for God are like liquid myrrh dripping from my fingers while the door to oneness stays locked to Jesus.

I have learned that the ways I chose to cope with pain and fear in my life became the veils which obscured my vision of Jesus. Though they offered me covering and temporary safety, these veils became walls which closed me in and shut me off from the help to be found in His presence. I had to let the veils go to receive His help in those painful places in my heart.

I have learned I cannot improve my situation by improving myself. I can only lay my heart open. Yes, it is scary, but the Person to whom I am opening my heart is not scary. Looking into His face, seeing the light of God combined with the sensitivity of a Man who has experienced the struggles inherent in humanity, causes me to lose my fear. More than that, I am enthralled.

I found that what the bride described about Him became all I could see. I saw gentle eyes turned upon me, filled with mystery and tender understanding. I saw torn flesh like carved ivory taking the pain, the fear, and the power to hurt out of the most horrific situations I have ever been exposed to. I saw nail-pierced hands holding open the passage into Father's arms for me. And I saw a face open and inviting, and eyes alight with love, welcoming me into His embrace.

This is the Person we seek. But where are we to find Him? As the bride discovered, He does not hide. The place we find Him is the place He has always been found.

It was in the garden that He walked with Adam in the cool of the day. There He shared His heart and listened as the man and woman shared theirs with Him. It was then that man had oneness with God - unity, intimacy. It was a literal place on earth. And though Eden has been closed to us, Jesus said, "My kingdom is not of this world" (John 18:36, NKJV, *paraphrased*), and, "The kingdom of God is within you" (Luke 17:21, NKJV, *paraphrased*). This is where God waits for us to join Him day by day.

What was it that made Eden heaven on earth? What changed and caused man to lose his closeness to God? Do you remember?

We say the word "sin" with so little comprehension. Yes, they sinned. And you may be like me – for I want to blame them, at least a little. But what did they do?

They questioned God's goodness. They doubted His kind intentions toward them. They reached for something to satisfy a taste and found it was an empty promise after all. They very soon realized their error, but the door had been closed and only Jesus could reopen it.

Eden was like heaven, because all that was there was what God wanted there. His will was present on earth even as it is in heaven. Adam and Eve lived in the rest of God. There was no end to the day God ceased from His works and all creation rested in Him. Hebrews 4 describes this rest as the place we are meant to live our life in God.

I have been thinking a lot about the garden since I began to understand its significance. As a result, I have been experiencing a new level of freedom. I believe I have found a key to truly live every day in the peace and joy of His presence.

In the beginning Eden was the place man walked with God. Everything there flowed from God's heart. It was a place of unbroken fellowship with Him and unquestioned trust in His goodness. Man lost that fellowship when he believed the lie that there was something worth having outside of God's provision for him.

Adam ate the fruit and was changed by what he had done. The tree of life was also in the garden. The thought that Adam would eat from that tree and then live forever in the condition of separation from God was too terrible to contemplate. God didn't take Eden away from man. In His goodness, He sent man away from Eden – for a while.

Four thousand years go by. We are shown another garden. In John 19:41-42 (NKJV), we find, "Now in the place where He was crucified there was a garden, and in the garden a new tomb in which no one had yet been laid. So there they laid Jesus . . ."

I have never seen God do anything without a purpose. When sin caused the death of the first man and all who followed after him, it happened in a garden. The original garden was the scene where our access to eternal life was cut off.

When Jesus became sin for us and put sin to death, all that had been lost was restored to us. Jesus took our death and left it with His grave clothes lying in His tomb. His tomb, which was also the place of His resurrection, was in a garden. Jesus' death and resurrection restored our access to the tree of life.

Living in the garden with God is not complicated. There is only one thing to be settled in our hearts. It is whether or not we believe God is good. Once we decide He is truly good, all that is left is to gather up all our doubts, fears, and desires, and present them to Him. Eve's mistake was in believing there was something good to be had apart from God. We can live every day in the joy of His presence if we reverse that lie within our own hearts.

The bride recalls, "He feeds his flock in the gardens, and he gathers lilies," and "He feeds his flock among the lilies."

Jesus talked about lilies when He said, ". . . Consider the lilies of the field . . . they neither toil nor spin; and yet I say to you that even Solomon in all his glory was not arrayed like one of these" (Matthew 6:28-29, NKJV).

What are we to learn from the lilies? They toil not, yet they are clothed in glory. Lilies represent quietness of heart, trust toward God, resting in the settled understanding of God's kind intentions toward us. The bridegroom will be found in the garden among the lilies.

The word which is translated "feeds his flock" is "ra'ah." It is a word which means to tend a flock, but it also means to associate with a friend. Therefore, this passage could be paraphrased, "My beloved has gone to his garden, where all that is to be found in heart and hands is open toward him. There he will be found in company with his friends; those who have learned to trust his heart. I am my beloved's, and my beloved is mine. He meets me, and satisfies every need within me as I set my heart to trust in his goodness and to rest in his love."

It is our Bridegroom's desire that we rest in His peace. He does not stop in His pursuit of us until we come into the astounding fullness of that rest.

PURSUIT AND REST

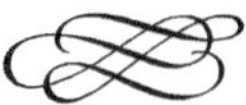

With an overflowing heart the bridegroom concludes this section with seven verses describing the woman who is the delight of his soul. He says,

"O my love, you are as beautiful as Tirzah, lovely as Jerusalem, awesome as an army with banners! Turn your eyes away from me, for they have overcome me. Your hair is like a flock of goats going down from Gilead. Your teeth are like a flock of sheep which have come up from the washing; every one bears twins, and none is barren among them. Like a piece of pomegranate are your temples behind your veil. There are sixty queens and eighty concubines, and virgins without number. My dove, my perfect one, is the only one, the only one of her mother, the favorite of the one who bore her. The daughters saw her and called her blessed. The queens and the concubines, and they praised her. Who is she who looks forth as the morning, fair as the moon, clear as the sun, awesome as an army with banners?" (Song 6:4-10).

"O my love, you are as beautiful as Tirzah" (Song 6:4).

HUNDREDS OF YEARS BEFORE JOSHUA LED THE ISRAELITES INTO CANAAN, a man named Abram responded to the voice of God. I imagine he appeared much like the other men of his generation, but in Abram there was a rare and wonderful quality. In Abram God found a man who listened for His voice. He became God's friend. God blessed Abram (whose name meant 'exalted father'), renamed him Abraham (father of a multitude), and made a promise to him that in his offspring all of the earth would be blessed (Genesis 12:3 & 17:5).

Fast forward nearly five hundred years to the days when Moses was portioning out the Promised Land to the children of Israel. There was a man of the tribe of Manasseh who had five daughters, but no son. His name was Zelophehad. Zelophehad died in the wilderness before the land was divided among the tribes. Believing that the promise of blessing upon Abraham was to all of his descendants, in an unprecedented act, the daughters of Zelophehad requested, and were granted, an allotment of land since their father had no son to inherit his portion (Numbers 27:1-12).

Tirzah was one of the daughters of Zelophehad who pursued her inheritance in Israel. She wanted a place in the household of faith as a descendant of Abraham. Tirzah sought the portion that was rightfully hers, but which would not have come to her without her pursuit. The heart within her was the same heart that led Abram out of Ur and into a lifetime of wandering the land which was to become the land of Israel.

Tirzah's portion became a city in the hill country west of the Jordan. It was known for its beautiful situation, but a city is not merely about buildings or landscapes. A city is about the people it represents. When the bridegroom said of his bride that she is "as beautiful as Tirzah" he was expressing the pleasure he has in her willingness to push beyond limitations until she comes into the fullness of what rightfully belongs to her.

"Lovely as Jerusalem" (Song 6:4).

Tirzah is beautiful to God because she sought a place in Him. Jerusalem is beautiful to God because He found in her a place for Himself. The word translated "lovely" is "naveh" which means suitable or beautiful. The root of this word is "na'ah," which means, "to be at home."

The prophet, Ezekiel, recorded a vision of the glory of God filling the temple in Jerusalem as He came to live amongst His people. God said, ". . . Son of man, *this* is the place of My throne and the place of the soles of My feet, where I will dwell in the midst of the children of Israel forever" (Ezekiel 43:7a, NKJV).

These are not words of condescension, but of desire. It was God's desire to dwell amongst His people. It is His greatest desire to make His home in your heart and mine. He delights to bring us into oneness with Himself so that He may share all He is with us.

The bride is seen in Revelation 21 as the New Jerusalem coming down out of the clouds. In this picture she represents those who have flung wide their hearts' doors and have given God full access to their souls. These have trusted in His goodness and entered into His rest. In the city which is called "the bride" our Bridegroom will dwell with His people forever.

Lovely is Jerusalem, the city God calls home.

"As beautiful as Tirzah, lovely as Jerusalem" are words which vibrate with the joy and longing of one who has yearned for his home through many long years. This may amaze us, but there is more. The bridegroom now describes his bride as "awesome as an army with banners" (Song 6:4).

The bride is occupied with the person of her bridegroom. With her attention focused on his wonderful attributes, she is unaware that she has moved into a dynamic place. Her rest amidst the lilies has become a place of magnificent power. The bride's vision is filled with her bridegroom, but the enemies of the bridegroom see in her his awesome power which is capable of destroying their evil deeds.

The word "awesome" does not merely speak of a wonderful thing, but is a word which means: to frighten, to be frightful or terrible. The presence of the banners indicates the bride is wholly identified with her bridegroom. She is under his authority and moves in his governmental power. The bride has come to rest in the heart of her bridegroom and in that place has become a dread army to his enemies.

A PARADOX

The bridegroom then says, "Turn your eyes away
from me for they have overcome me" (Song 6:5).

"Turn your eyes away," is like stop, don't stop. What he sees there is more than he can stand, but it is a gift too wonderful to cease taking in. Overcome in the original language is "rahab," which means: to urge, importune, or capture.

Here is an amazing thing. The bride has come to a place of absolute rest in the goodness of her bridegroom. She has let go of all thoughts of self-protection and self-provision. She trusts him to consider all her needs and care for all that is important to her, and he says, "Your eyes have overcome me." Her eyes are like deep wells revealing what is in her soul. Her bridegroom is captivated by her eyes. What he sees there compels him to do all that is within his power to satisfy her unspoken desires.

I remember saying in the infancy of my walk with the Lord that I wanted to have power with God. I wasn't looking to control Him, but

I wanted to influence Him so miracles would happen when I prayed. I have walked with the Lord for many years, and have seen many answers to prayer, but the power with God I once desired is no longer the object I pursue. I love to see the miraculous, but now it is God's pleasure I seek. The object of my prayers is to find the thing God wants to do, the thing that will bring Him the greatest joy, and lay hold of it. Here I also find His power.

It is a paradox which is explained in this passage. The bride has great influence with her bridegroom when she learns to place absolute trust in his kindness. He says her eyes urge him, importune him; yet she wasn't asking for anything. She was merely being there, loving him, and by her position in the earth she presented to him the things that mattered to her.

Can love move the heart of God? Come and see . . .

Early one morning a grief-stricken woman stood beside a garden tomb. Three days before, the unimaginable had happened. Roman soldiers, at the urging of the Jewish leaders, had crucified the Person who embodied love. She had stayed all day on the hill called "the place of the skull," and watched the torturous execution of the kindest Man she had ever known. She came now to the place where His body was buried, wishing only to be near Him for a while.

Mary had cried so much since that terrible day, it was a wonder she had any tears left within her. But when she reached the garden tomb, another shock brought a fresh wave of grief. The stone was rolled away from the entrance of the tomb, and the body of her Lord was gone.

No! It was too much. Even what little comfort she would have had from weeping at His grave was now to be denied her. She bent to look inside the tomb and saw two men dressed in white sitting where His body had lain. They asked her why she wept, and she answered, "Because they have taken away my Lord, and I do not know where they have laid Him."

Then she turned and saw a Man standing beside her, who said, "Woman, why are you weeping? Whom are you seeking?"

She thought He was the gardener and answered, "Sir, if you have carried Him away, tell me where you have laid Him, and I will take Him away."

Then Jesus called her name, "Mary!"

At that she realized who He was and reached for Him as she joyfully cried, "Teacher!"

But Jesus said to her, "Do not cling to Me, for I have not yet ascended to My Father; but go to My brethren and say to them, I am ascending to My Father and your Father, and to My God and your God" (John 20:1-18, NKJV, *paraphrased*).

Can love move the heart of God?

Jesus interrupted His ascension into heaven to comfort a woman who loved Him with all of her being. She just wanted to be near Him. She wasn't asking for anything more. She loved Him. It was all that mattered to her. Her love positioned her to be the first to learn the message that would change the world. Death did not keep Him. He is alive!

HEARTS AT HOME

"Your hair is like a flock of goats going down from Gilead.
Your teeth are like a flock of sheep which have come up from the
washing; every one bears twins, and none is barren among them.
Like a piece of pomegranate are your temples behind your veil"
(Song 6:5-7).

Here the bridegroom restates the description he had given of the bride in a previous passage. Earlier he had named seven attributes of his bride, giving a deeply moving metaphoric description of each. He now renews his words regarding three of her attributes: her hair, teeth, and temples.

The bridegroom describes her hair, the glory of her head, like the mountain goats which easily trip like a rippling brook down the sides of Gilead, a mount which had served as a refuge to God's people in perilous times.

He speaks of her teeth as soft and gentle creatures, white and clean.

He states they are fruitful, everyone bearing twins, showing evidence of great blessing.

And he declares her temples are like a piece of pomegranate, the fruit which more than any other emphasizes its seeds. Pomegranates represent unlimited fruitfulness. Saying her temples are like a piece of pomegranate is reminiscent of Abraham looking at the stars and seeing the number of his descendants. Who can count them?

In these three attributes, the bridegroom is emphasizing the home they have found in their love together. The love they share is a place of comfort and a joyful resting place. Her words come forth from the abundance of her heart in purity and gentleness. Her thoughts abound with faith-filled truth, holding the promise of fruitfulness far beyond the time she will leave this world.

The bridegroom has drawn a picture with his words of his bride's heart as a place of refreshing and repose. Her heart is trustworthy. She will not betray him. She will honor him in all of her ways. That which issues from her heart is confirmed in the gentle life-giving words that have been bathed in cleansing truth. She has learned to believe the kind intentions of his heart toward her. She has gained an eternal kingdom perspective. Now she constantly looks to him full of expectancy, and he is able to answer her with limitless abundance.

THE ONLY ONE

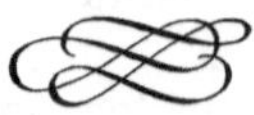

"There are sixty queens and eighty concubines,
and virgins without number. My dove, my perfect one,
is the only one. The only one of her mother.
The favorite of the one who bore her" (Song 6:8-9).

"*Sixty queens...*"

Sixty is a number which (as six times ten) speaks of a righteous man. In the gateways of the temple in Ezekiel's vision (Ezekiel 40), we find the gateposts are sixty cubits high. Nowhere else in the vision do we find the number sixty; but finding it as the height of the gateposts reminds me that in John 10:7 Jesus called Himself the door of the sheep.

Those who are queens have entered through the door. A queen is a royal person. She stands in a place of authority next to the king. I believe in this passage "sixty queens" refers to those in the household of faith who have learned to walk in the authority that belongs to believers. They stand within the door and minister on the Lord's behalf.

"Eighty concubines . . ."

Eighty is the multiple of eight times ten which speaks of the righteousness of a circumcised heart. The eighth day of life was the day of circumcision. It marked the cutting away of the flesh; allegorically speaking of the fallen nature which hinders the life of God in us. Eight is the number we associate with a new beginning, the new beginning of a life consecrated to God. Concubines are servants. They represent those of the household of faith who love God and have committed their lives to serving Him.

"Virgins without number . . ."

Virgins are those who have not experienced physical intimacy. In this reference, I believe they refer to those who are new in the faith, or those who have believed the word of life, but have not pursued more in the knowledge of God than the basic truth of salvation. These are innumerable.

"But my dove, my perfect one is the only one."

The bride is unique. She is the only one, the favorite.

Does God have a favorite? I believe He does. Does His favoritism exclude anyone? Not if they want Him. God's favoritism embraces the heart of any man or woman, boy or girl who wants to love God in the way that goes beyond merely believing like the virgins, or serving like the concubines, or even acting on His behalf and speaking for Him in the earth like the queens. "The dove, the perfect one" represents all of those who are overcome with His beauty and His holiness. These are those who want His presence more than their own breath.

She is one: 'echad. The Hebrew word for "one" is used three times in this verse. She is the only 'echad; the 'echad of her mother; the favorite 'echad of the one who bore her.

Finding a place where the word 'echad is used three times together to describe the bride is like happening upon the source of the river of life. Here is a doorway into the heart of God which is filled with mystery and meaning.

The most significant passage in the Old Testament is what the Jewish people call "the Shema." Jesus referred to it as the greatest commandment. It embodies all that we need to walk in relationship with God.

We find it in Deuteronomy 6:4-5 (NKJV): "Hear O Israel: The LORD our God, the Lord is one ('echad)! You shall love the Lord your God with all your heart, with all your soul, and with all your strength."

"The Lord our God, the Lord is one!" As I type these words, I am overwhelmed by an awareness of His holiness. I feel this is too sacred to speak of, so I stop and wait and listen. Then the Holy Spirit nudges me to continue. Trembling in awe, my heart prostrate before Him, I write:

> "The Lord" (YHWH): I Am. God told Moses, "My Name is I Am That I Am" (Exodus 3:14, NKJV). YHWH, or Yahweh, is translated: The Lord.

> "Our God" (Elohiym): A plural form of the word which speaks of God in His fullness.

> "The Lord is one!" ('Echad): one, a unit, united, in unity. God is one.

Jesus said, "I and My Father are one" (John 10:38, NKJV). Agreement between them is absolute. There is no discord. No rebellion. No doubting the goodness of heart or will. There are no fractures or fissures between them which would make room for decay in even the smallest measure. They are whole. Together they are one.

Now the bridegroom uses this word three times to describe the bride. Three is the number of the triune God. Three uses of 'echad indicates the bride has not only entered into oneness, but into holiness – oneness with God.

"The daughters saw her and called her blessed." "Ashar," the Hebrew word for blessed, is also translated: happy, prosperous, successful, and contented. The daughters called her "happy, successful, contented." If this is an open door before me, why would I not choose it?

The bride's unity with her bridegroom is further seen in the description of her given by the queens and concubines. "The queens and the concubines, and they praised her, 'Who is she who looks forth as the morning, fair as the moon, clear as the sun?'" (Song 6:9-10).

Jesus promised that He would give the morning star to those who overcome (Revelation 2:28). Later, Jesus says, "I am the Root and Offspring of David, the Bright and Morning Star" (Revelation 22:16, NKJV).

The bride is filled with the light of the morning, the night, and the day. She is one with Him who is both "the Morning Star" and "the Sun of Righteousness, who rises with healing in His wings" (Malachi 4:2, NKJV).

The bride is seen as one who carries within her the expectation and joy of the dawn, the light which illuminates the darkest nights, and the warmth and truth of the light of day. It is clear to all who see her, she is blessed.

But there is one other description of the bride given here. The women repeat the bridegroom's words that she is "awesome as an army with banners" (Song 6:10). As the bride remains in the garden among the lilies, her bridegroom's banners fly above her in a display of identity which makes her a terror to his enemies and a power on the earth. His banners are the evidence of his dominion. The bride is under his protection. His banner over her is his love.

How did the bride arrive at this place?

She left her self-protective veils, her personal righteousness, and her careful religion behind, and pursued her bridegroom with all of her heart. When she was asked to describe him, she remembered his incomparable goodness and his inescapable love. With the memory of his goodness filling her mind, she turned her heart wholly toward him and found herself surrounded by lilies in his garden. Now with a trusting and quiet heart, she is resting in his kind intentions toward her.

As the bride recounted her bridegroom's attributes, a transformation took place. She was changed from ragged to royal. I like to picture this as the time when Cinderella got her ball gown. The dress she once wore, her best efforts at beauty, torn and soiled by the things which she suffered, have been miraculously transformed into royal robes to which even Solomon in all of his glory cannot compare.

The bridegroom's description of his bride leaves no doubt of his love for her. She is one with him in heart and soul. She is the answer to his heart's desire. Clothed in the light of his glory, she carries his image wherever she goes.

PART V

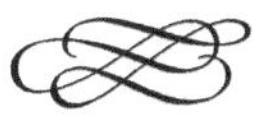

SONG OF SOLOMON 6:11 - 8:4, NKJV

"I went down to the garden of nuts
To see the verdure of the valley,
To see whether the vine had budded
And the pomegranates had bloomed.
Before I was even aware,
My soul had made me
As the chariots of my noble people.

Return, return, O Shulamite;
Return, return, that we may look upon you!

What would you see in the Shulamite –
As it were, the dance of the two camps?

How beautiful are your feet in sandals,
O prince's daughter!
The curves of your thighs are like jewels,
The work of the hands of a skillful workman.
Your navel is a rounded goblet;

It lacks no blended beverage.
Your waist is a heap of wheat
Set about with lilies.
Your two breasts are like two fawns,
Twins of a gazelle.
Your neck is like an ivory tower,
Your eyes like the pools in Heshbon
By the gate of Bath Rabbim.
Your nose is like the tower of Lebanon
Which looks toward Damascus.
Your head crowns you like Carmel,
And the hair of your head is like purple;
A king is held captive by your tresses.

How fair and how pleasant you are,
O love, with your delights!
This stature of yours is like a palm tree,
And your breasts like its clusters.
I said, 'I will go up to the palm tree,
I will take hold of its branches.'
Let now your breasts be like
Clusters of the vine,
The fragrance of your breath like apples,
And the roof of your mouth like the best wine.

The wine goes down smoothly for my beloved,
Moving gently the lips of sleepers.
I am my beloved's
And his desire is toward me.

Come, my beloved,
Let us go forth to the field;
Let us lodge in the villages.
Let us get up early to the vineyards;
Let us see if the vine has budded,

Whether the grape blossoms are open,
And the pomegranates are in bloom.
There I will give you my love.
The mandrakes give off a fragrance,
And at our gates are pleasant fruits,
All manner, new and old,
Which I have laid up for you, my beloved.

Oh, that you were like my brother,
Who nursed at my mother's breasts!
If I should find you outside,
I would kiss you;
I would not be despised,
I would lead you and bring you
Into the house of my mother,
She who used to instruct me.
I would cause you to drink of spiced wine,
Of the juice of my pomegranate.

His left hand is under my head,
And his right hand embraces me.
I charge you, O daughters of Jerusalem,

Do not stir up nor awaken love until it pleases."

BECOMING

*L*ike the psalmist who said, "Return to your rest, O my soul, for the Lord has dealt bountifully with you" (Psalm 116:7, NKJV), the bride has come to rest in the garden by bringing all her heart into agreement with the heart of her bridegroom. She no longer troubles herself with the worries which once disturbed her peace. She knows whose she is: "I am my beloved's," she said. She is at rest in this truth.

Now her attention is turned toward the fruit of her garden. "I went down to the garden of nuts to see the verdure of the valley, to see whether the vine had budded and the pomegranates had bloomed" (Song 6:11).

The valley mentioned here in Hebrew is "nachalah." It is the word for a narrow valley, a brook, a river, or a torrent. The river of God in Ezekiel's vision (chapter 47) that flows from the threshold of the temple is also "nachalah." The root is "nachal" which means: to inherit, to possess, to take as a heritage, or to occupy. The bride is exploring her inheritance.

The three fruits the bride is looking for in the garden are nuts, grapes, and pomegranates. Because one of the best ways to understand Scripture is to compare it with Scripture, I looked for other places where the fruits mentioned here play a key role. I remembered the almond branch in Jeremiah 1, and the vine in John 15. The pomegranates are about multiplication, so I thought of Abraham looking at the stars. Let us see if these references help with this passage.

Although the nut mentioned here is a generic word meaning "nut," I believe we could safely say that a nut orchard in Israel would contain almonds. In the first chapter of Jeremiah, God is commissioning Jeremiah to speak on His behalf. Jeremiah has questions about God's choice, so in order to convince him, God asks, "Jeremiah, what do you see?" Jeremiah answers, "I see a branch of an almond tree." Then the Lord says, "You have seen well, for I am watching over My word to perform it" (Jeremiah 1:11-12, NKJV, *paraphrased*).

How do almonds indicate the promise of the faithfulness of God? In Hebrew the two words are similar. "Shaqad" is the word for watching. "Shaqed" is the word for almond. But, even more importantly, almonds are the earliest blooming tree. In Hebrew culture they are called "the waker," because they diligently watch for the spring.

Another passage where God uses almonds to indicate His faithful diligence is recorded in Numbers 17. The children of Israel had followed Moses out of Egypt, but some of them were dissatisfied with his leadership and wanted to choose their own leaders. They said to Moses and Aaron, "You take too much upon yourselves, for all the congregation is holy" (Numbers 16:3, NKJV, *paraphrased*).

To settle the question, God told Moses to place twelve rods before Him in the tent of meeting. Each rod would represent a tribe of Israel. In the morning, the rod that belonged to Aaron (Moses' tribe) had budded, blossomed, and produced almonds.

The bride says, "I went down to the garden of nuts to see the verdure of the valley." She is expecting fruitfulness. She doesn't wonder *if* there will be fruit. She goes to see what fruit is there. God is watching over His word to perform it. God has made it clear she is His. His banner flies above her. His almonds bloom and bear fruit within her. He has given her a "nachalah," a possession in Him. He is committed to her. He is Faithful.

"To see whether the vine had budded (or flourished) . . ."

Let us at John's Gospel, chapter 15. Jesus said, "I am the true vine, and My Father is the vinedresser. Every branch in Me that does not bear fruit He takes away; and every branch that bears fruit He prunes, that it may bear more fruit" (John 15:1-2, NKJV). What is translated here as "takes away" is "airo." The Greek meaning of "airo" is: to lift, raise, bear up, carry, loose, remove, take away. The translators gave "airo" the meaning "take away," but we could as easily see it saying that when a branch does not bear fruit, He lifts it up. Understanding that the heart of God is to save, I think it is reasonable to think that what He does for one who is struggling is to pick them up and carry them.

Jesus goes on to say, "Abide in Me, and I in you. As the branch cannot bear fruit of itself, unless it abides in the vine, neither can you, unless you abide in Me. I am the vine, you are the branches. He who abides in Me, and I in him, bears much fruit; for without Me you can do nothing" (John 15:4-5, NKJV).

The bride is looking for fruit on the vine. She has an expectation for good because of His relationship with her. Jesus promises we will bear fruit as we live in connection to Him. If we are struggling to find enough light to flourish, His Father will lift us up and carry us until we are strong. But, He says, we must remain in Him, for a branch cut off from the vine will not bear fruit no matter how strong or healthy it once was. Jesus is the Source of our life. We never outgrow our need of Him.

Like the vine, the bride has found her life in Him. Now she lives in joyful expectation of experiencing the goodness which flows from His life.

> "And the pomegranates had bloomed . . ."

Pomegranates are a fruit full of seeds. Like God telling Abraham to look at the stars and count them if he was able saying, "so shall your descendants be" (Genesis 15:5, NKJV), the presence of pomegranates indicates both the surety and expanse of the promises of God. As we discovered before, pomegranates are found at the entrance of the temple and on the hem of the high priest's robe. They are consistently used to speak of limitless life in the presence of God.

We are fond of remembering Abraham as the father of faith, but I wonder if that is God's favorite view of him. I think, above all else, Abraham is God's friend. It was his friendship with God that caused him to believe. When we love someone and are sure of their character, as Abraham felt toward God, it isn't difficult to trust their word. Yes, Abraham believed God, and his faith gave God an open door into the affairs of men which has continued until this day. But more than Abraham's faith, I believe God would emphasize their friendship.

Abraham loved God and God loved Abraham. God gave His promise to His friend. The covenant they made together was a result of the love between them. Like the presence of the pomegranates in the garden, the promise of blessing and limitless multiplication upon Abraham's life was the fruit of intimacy born of love.

So, what do we see in the fruit of the garden? The bride is looking for increase in three things: nuts, vines, and pomegranates. Almonds speak of a heart which places trust in the faithful interest of God. The vine is all about the expectation for good as we entrust our lives to His care. And the pomegranates – ah, the pomegranates! They are all about friendship with God – loving Him, believing Him, and living in relationship with Him.

Her preoccupation with nurturing her garden has the bride unaware of the changes happening within her. While the bridegroom watches over her, the bride makes sure her heart is wholly turned toward him diligently nurturing her faith. She delights in the life she shares with

him and daily looks for the goodness which comes from his hand –
nurturing her hope. But most of all, her heart overflows with joy in
his love for her. She spends every day discovering ways to bring more
joy to him – nurturing her love. The fruit of the bride's garden represents her faith, her hope, and her love.

Engaged in these delightful and absorbing activities as she is, the bride
doesn't even notice the change in her station. Like the "Ugly Duck-
ling" who one day discovers he is a swan, the woman who had once
told her bridegroom not to look at her because she was "dark" now
finds herself set upon the chariots of the nobility. Her desire to love
her bridegroom with everything within her has transported her to
this place of honor among those who are intimates of the king; the
Ammi Nadib, the nobility who surround his throne.

CROWNED WITH HONOR

"Before I was even aware, my soul had made me
as the chariots of my noble people" (Song 6:12).

This translation says, "my soul," but the word can also mean: desire, heart, or pleasure. The word for "made" can also mean: to place, convey, or set on. So we could read this as the bride saying, "Before I was even aware, my heart's desire conveyed me to the chariots of the nobility."

The noble people are the Ammi Nadib. The original language describes them as willing hearted people, noble princes, people who are magnanimous, generous, and free.

Dear friend, it has happened again. I am astonished by the place into which this study has led me. I have looked and thought, "This can't be right. What I think I'm seeing can't be right; it's too fantastic." But as I have compared the Scriptures, and waited before the Lord, I have been required to acknowledge it as truth.

I think David must have seen this, because he said, "What is man that you are mindful of him? Or the son of man that you visit him? You have made him a little lower than the angels. You have crowned him with glory and honor" (Psalm 8:4-5, NKJV).

The writer to the Hebrews quotes this passage from Psalms in Hebrews 2:6-7, and then continues in verse 9, "But we see Jesus, who was made a little lower than the angels for the suffering of death, crowned with glory and honor, that He by the grace of God might taste death for everyone" (NKJV).

Our life is in Jesus. He tasted death for us, and the glory which belongs to Him He has given to us. But what does this mean? What is this glory we are given to share? It was the study of the chariots of the noble people that has taken me on this fantastic journey through Scripture. I will try to share it with you.

There are two Hebrew words which are translated chariot. One refers to the vehicle drawn by horses. The other speaks of riding either on horseback or on a chariot.

God's chariot is pictured in both the tabernacle and the temple and was seen by the prophet Ezekiel and John the apostle. His chariot bears His glory. We are invited into His chariot through the death and resurrection of Jesus. Through Jesus' sacrifice, we are invited into the weighty, holy glory of God.

How can this be? God has been very kind to give us pictures of these spiritual truths in the layout and furnishings used in the tabernacle which Moses made in the wilderness, and in the temple which David's son, Solomon, built in Jerusalem.

In 1 Chronicles 28:11-18 (NKJV) we read, "Then David gave his son Solomon the plans for the vestibule, its houses, its treasuries, its upper chambers, its inner chambers, and the place of the mercy seat; and the plans for all that he had by the Spirit, of the courts of the house of the Lord . . . He gave gold by weight for things of gold, for all articles used in every kind of service . . . and refined gold by weight for the altar of incense, and for *the construction of the chariot, that is, the gold cherubim that spread their wings and overshadowed the ark of the covenant of the Lord (emphasis mine).*

"All this," David says in verse 19, "the Lord made me understand in writing, by His hand upon me, all the works (or details) of these plans."

We find the presence of cherubim wherever the glory of God is manifested. Cherubim in Ezekiel's vision of God appeared as four living creatures having familiar features, yet unlike anything he had ever seen. He describes their appearance: faces, wings, legs, feet, hands, and the wheel within a wheel which was present with each of them. Then he says, "As for the likeness of the living creatures, their appearance was like burning coals of fire, like the appearance of torches going back and forth among the living creatures. The fire was bright, and out of the fire went lightening" (Ezekiel 1:13, NKJV).

It was David who spoke of God in Psalm 18:10 (NKJV) saying, "And He rode upon a cherub, and flew; He flew upon the wings of the wind."

When Elijah was taken to heaven, 2 Kings 2:11 (NKJV) states: "A chariot of fire appeared with horses of fire, and Elijah went up by a whirlwind into heaven."

Also in Isaiah 66:15 (NKJV) we read: "For behold, the Lord will come with fire and with His chariots, like a whirlwind."

The description of the living beings is in such detail there can be no mistaking Ezekiel was seeing in reality what had been given by revelation to Moses and David. The Ark of the Covenant was made with golden cherubim, and we are told the mercy seat between (or amidst) the cherubim is the place where God meets with man. The apostle John tells us Jesus Himself is the Mercy Seat (1 John 2:2 & 4:10).

Ezekiel was amazed by the appearance of the cherubim, but they were not present on their own. In Ezekiel 1:26 (NKJV) we read, "And above the firmament over their heads was the likeness of a throne, in appearance like a sapphire stone; on the likeness of the throne was a likeness with the appearance of a man high above it."

In the next verses he describes the man's fiery appearance and the rainbow which was all around Him. Then he finishes by saying, "This was the appearance of the likeness of the glory of the Lord" (Ezekiel 1:28, NKJV).

Seeing all of this brings new meaning to Paul's letter to the Ephesians and his assertion that we have been chosen by God to become His children, holy and blameless before Him, to the praise of the glory of His grace. God loves us so much He has made us alive with Christ, raised us up, and made us sit together in the heavenly places in Christ Jesus (Ephesians 1:3-6 & 2:4-6).

Can you now understand my astonishment? God hasn't merely saved us and given us a place in heaven. He has seated us with Him in glory – with Jesus amidst the cherubim.

The bride says her heart's desire conveyed her to the chariots of the nobility. The desire of her heart was to be with her bridegroom and to give him her love. She wasn't aware of the change in her position as it was taking place. She was absorbed in loving her bridegroom. It is this very heart attitude that worked the transformation which caused her to be seated with him in his chariot.

Our hunger prepares us to enter into the weightiness of His presence. We are drawn to His presence by our desire to be near Him. Without conscious thought, we draw closer and closer with increasing boldness, then one day we look up and realize we are sitting with Him, surrounded by His glory.

As I was thinking of this passage, I remembered a vision I once had when the Lord lifted me up on a horse with Him. I can still feel the lunge of the horse as it began to run. I remember feeling the power of the animal. It was a very strong animal. I remember the wind against my face and in my hair, and the feeling of strong arms holding me steady against a firm chest. I felt safe and exhilarated and thrilled to be on an adventure with Him. I remember sensing His joy in my company, and at the same time feeling amazed that He had chosen me.

This vision did not happen because I was seeking to be seated with Him. It came at a time when I had been praying to identify lies I had believed which were hindering my trust in His goodness. I had been seeking to make my heart completely open and vulnerable to Him. The vision was His response to my repentance. As I renounced the lies which had been keeping my heart separated from His, He responded by taking me up to ride with Him. It is a ride which has yet to end.

THE DANCE OF THE TWO CAMPS

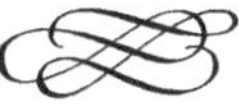

"Return, return, O Shulamite; return, return,
that we may look upon you!" (Song 6:13).

The daughters of Jerusalem now see something in the bride that is both intriguing and attractive. They call her by the feminine version of Solomon's name, indicating that they recognize her union with him. While the bride is absorbed with her bridegroom, the daughters of Jerusalem don't seem to be seeing him. It is the bride who has caught their attention. They want to look at her, talk to her; discover what has brought this change.

But the bride is not interested in talking about herself. Her answer indicates her astonishment at their interest in her when someone as notable and wonderful as her bridegroom is present. She answers them by saying, "What would you see in the Shulamite – as it were, the dance of the two camps?" (Song 6:13).

"The dance of the two camps" explains the transformation which has so obviously caught the attention of the daughters of Jerusalem. The bride points them to an historical event which their people celebrated with a dance called Mahanaim, or the dance of the two camps. This event is recorded in Genesis 32.

Isaac, the long-awaited son of Abraham, fathered twin sons. Even at their birth the stage is set for the unfolding drama of their lives. Esau was the firstborn, but Jacob, born immediately following, was holding onto his brother's heel. They named him "Jacob" which means supplanter, or one who takes the place of another by force or trickery. It was a prophecy of their lives.

Esau, as the firstborn, was entitled to the blessing of Abraham's promise: "In your seed all of the nations of the earth will be blessed" (Genesis 22:18a, NKJV). He cared little for this heritage, while Jacob hungered for it and watched for a way to claim it for himself. One day the opportunity came. Through trickery, and with his mother's help, he gained his father's blessing. Then fearing the wrath of his brother, Jacob ran away to the house of his mother's brother.

Jacob stayed with Laban for twenty years. While there, he married Laban's two daughters, and fathered eleven sons and a daughter. God blessed Laban's household because of Jacob. Laban was aware it was through the favor of God on Jacob that his flocks and herds increased, but he also saw that same favor caused the greater wealth to go to Jacob. Laban, who was as conniving as Jacob, changed Jacob's wages ten times in an effort to divert the wealth toward himself. Finally, when Laban's attitude toward Jacob soured, God told Jacob it was time to go home.

Jacob gathered up his household and left secretly; but when Laban discovered they were gone, he pursued them. From the confrontation which followed, the two men struck a covenant, an agreement that God would be the witness to their actions concerning one another. At that time, "Jacob swore by the Fear of his father Isaac," which indicated he feared the God of his father, but that God was *his father's* God (Genesis 31:53).

Jacob and his family traveled on, but as they drew near to his home an event took place which would change the course of Jacob's life. Jacob was returning with a vast company of people and animals, and as he arrived at a certain place, the angels of God met them. Jacob saw the angels, and Genesis 32:2 records Jacob as saying, "'This is God's camp.' And he called the name of that place 'Mahanaim'" (Literally, Double Camp).

Continuing on his journey, Jacob was afraid of the anger of his brother and sent messengers ahead with gifts of livestock. When he received word Esau was on his way to meet him with a company of four hundred men, Jacob prayed, reminding God that he was following His direction by returning, and asked for protection for himself and his family.

The night before Esau arrived, Jacob sent his wives and children on ahead while he remained by the brook Jabbok. There he wrestled all night with a Man. (The same Man of God who had visited his grandfather, Abraham, and had received Abraham's worship.)

I can only imagine what was in Jacob's heart that night. He knew what he had done; that it was robbery against his brother. God had led him, protected him, even blessed him, yet Jacob was still Jacob: supplanter, conniver, trickster. I believe the wrestling included the desire in Jacob's heart to be blessed as he was, to be justified in himself, but God had better things for Jacob.

As dawn approached, the Man saw Jacob was not giving in, so He touched the socket of his hip and put his hip out of joint. Then He said, "Let me go."

Jacob answered, "I will not let you go unless you bless me!"

The Man said, "What is your name?"

The moment of truth had arrived.

Jacob said, "My name is Jacob."

In that moment Jacob said in effect, "Uncle! I give up. I accede. I am who you say I am. I confess – I am a supplanter, a deceiver."

At this confession, I can almost hear God sigh, "At last!"

Now He can bless Jacob. Now He can do for him all that has been in His heart for him. The Man answered, ". . . Your name shall no longer be called Jacob, but Israel; for you have struggled with God and with men, and have prevailed" (Genesis 32:28, NKJV).

Israel the name given to Jacob comes from two Hebrew words meaning: to prevail, or rule as a prince, and God, the Almighty. Israel: Prince with God. This is the event which set the course for Israel from that day on. Jacob became Israel, his fathers' God became his own God, and his children celebrated the event with the Dance of the Mahanaim – the two camps in The Valley of the Angels.

The bride now acknowledges this same mercy upon her life in her response to the Daughters of Jerusalem. She knows her personal history: the way she has walked, the mistakes she has made, the desire to protect and justify herself. It is all there, just as it was in Jacob. And now she sees the kindness of God extended toward her. He has seated her with Him in His glory and crowned her as His bride. I cannot wonder at her response to the Daughters of Jerusalem. Why should they want to gaze at her, when they could see the King?

THE BRIDE

It is the bridegroom who gives the reason for the Daughters of Jerusalems' desire to look at the bride. In tender and passionate language, he describes the woman he loves:

"How beautiful are your feet in sandals, O prince's daughter!
The curves of your thighs are like jewels, the work of the hands
of a skillful workman.
Your navel is a rounded goblet; it lacks no blended beverage.
Your waist is a heap of wheat set about with lilies.
Your two breasts are like two fawns, twins of a gazelle.
Your neck is like an ivory tower,
Your eyes like the pools in Heshbon
by the gate of Bath Rabbim.
Your nose is like the tower of Lebanon
which looks toward Damascus.
Your head crowns you like Carmel,
And the hair of your head is like purple,
the king is held captive by your tresses.
How fair and how pleasant you are, O love, with your delights!

> This stature of yours is like a palm tree, and your breasts like its
> clusters. I said, "I will go up to the palm tree,
> I will take hold of its branches."
> Let now your breasts be like clusters of the vine,
> The fragrance of your breath like apples,
> And the roof of your mouth like the best wine" (Song 7:1-9).

On the wall of my husband's office hangs a portrait of Abraham Lincoln. When you stand across the room to view it, the shades of the picture blend to form a fair representation of his face; but when you step near, it becomes clear the artist built this image by assembling hundreds of tiny pictures of Abraham Lincoln, combining them in such a way that the lights and darks of the various pictures come together to display his image as one.

In this passage, we are being shown a portrait of the bride. For centuries she has been shrouded in mystery, yet in these days she is being revealed. She is one, yet her singleness is found in the assembly of millions. She is a multitude, yet each individual is seen, known, and loved as an individual. Each is essential to God, each is essential to form the whole, and each carries within them the likeness of Jesus our Lord.

As I began to write this part, I studied and researched and recorded what I found, but for a long time, the picture would not come into focus. Then one day as I sat with the Lord and pondered this passage, I realized this image is the bride through God's eyes. This is not what she says about herself, nor is it even something she fully understands. Her heart and soul have turned God-ward, and this is what He sees in her. The picture is a mystery, and the image will only become clear when she is viewed through eyes that see her through the love of God.

When the bride gave her description of the bridegroom (Song 5:10-15), she named twelve attributes. Twelve is the number that speaks of governmental authority. Now the bridegroom lists thirteen features of his bride. Thirteen attributes indicate she is abiding fully in her bridegroom's authority plus one and refers to "the greater works than these" which Jesus promised we would do (John 14:12). Thirteen is the number for double (or multiplied) anointing.

Here is a paradox. For centuries mankind has battled for supremacy through strength, violence, suppression, even annihilation. Yet now there is emerging upon the earth a people in whom the authority of heaven resides - for they are one with the one upon whose shoulders the government of creation rests.

In Isaiah 9:6-7 (NKJV) we read, "For unto us a Child is born, unto us a Son is given; and the government will be upon His shoulder. And His name will be called Wonderful Counselor, Mighty God, Everlasting Father, Prince of Peace. Of the increase of His government and peace there will be no end, upon the throne of David and over His kingdom, to order it and establish it with judgment and justice from that time forward, even forever. The zeal of the Lord of hosts will perform this."

The government of the kingdom of God rests upon the shoulders that bore the cross to Calvary, and the increase of that government is with those who love Him.

Jacob became Israel when he confessed his name, acknowledged his sin, and relinquished the ownership of his life; thereby making the exchange that would transform him from supplanter to prince with God. The bridegroom begins his description of the bride by calling her prince's daughter. She has identified herself with Jacob, has faced her own wrestling at Jabbok, and has been given a new name, and with it - a new identity.

She is no longer dark; burned by the sun. Now the light of the dawn, the sun, and the moon are in her being. She has become as awesome as an army with banners. Where she once looked to her bridegroom for a place to hide, to heal, and to find love, now a greater purpose for her life is being revealed.

Can a creature understand the heart of his Creator? May we enter the thoughts and feelings which brought about His actions as they relate to us? Do we even dare to consider ourselves capable of such an undertaking?

It is clear to me by the imprint of His fingertips upon everything I see that the King's scepter has been extended - inviting us near. He wants to reveal Himself to us. He wants us to see what is in His heart for us. The most gripping and compelling revelation of His heart for me is found in His love story. What has been hidden is ours to discover when we ponder the images He has given as windows into His heart.

Who is this bride who carries the authority of heaven in the earth?

We are being offered a picture of a woman in this passage. She is a woman, but much more than a woman. She is the bride of Christ. She is individually and collectively the people who have loved God and believed in the power of Jesus' blood for forgiveness of sin. She is the one who follows the Lamb and gives her life to Him even as He gives His life to her. She is holy by the power of Jesus' shed blood. She is His Ishshah; His Other-Just-The-Same.

Is this too far-fetched? Too fantastic to believe? Please think with me.

God made man in His image. Adam could find no companion suitable for himself among the animals. God caused a deep sleep to come upon Adam, took from his side a portion of his being, and built a woman. Adam was formed from the dust of the earth; formed as a sculptor works with clay. But the Bible says, woman was "banah"; built from the man's side. "Banah" is translated as "built," as to build an altar, to build a city, to build a house. She was made as a dwelling place is made.

When God brought the woman to the man, he called her his "Ishshah;" his "other-just-the-same." She was the one he had been looking for. She was his equal; the one who filled the empty place within him and satisfied his longing for companionship and love. In her was also his hope of salvation following their expulsion from the garden, for he called her "Eve – the mother of all living."

The man and the woman came together in the most intimate way two human beings may. Their union, their oneness, produced life, and God blessed their union and their fruitfulness, and promised salvation to mankind would come from this joining.

Is it not clear? Pan back with me and see ...

God, in timelessness, had created many beautiful beings, even those with the power to choose whether to serve Him, yet found no one suitable to be joined to Him. They were in a sense as the creatures to Adam; lovely, affectionate, loyal, but not the same.

God said, "Let Us make man in Our image and in Our likeness" (Genesis 1:26). Then, as only a Master Poet could, God formed the woman and brought her to the man, revealing through this His intention for mankind: oneness with Himself.

Throughout the history of Israel, God spoke of His people as His wife; He often used the symbolism of a house, a sanctuary, a dwelling place, and a city as a simile for this wife. Oneness has always been His goal. Holiness allows us to enter into oneness. He searches the earth for a holy people; a people who will be called by His name.

Although there were those who followed Him, the Ishshah was not found. Then God brought about a wound to the side of the Second Adam, His own Son; and from this wound poured the water and the blood from which would come the bride – the holy Ishshah. From the side of the first man, the woman was built. By the blood of the Savior, we are made holy; we become a "banah," a dwelling place for God.

Adam was joined to Eve and became one with her. Jesus prayed the night before He died for oneness, "I in them, and You in Me, that they may be made perfect in one" (John 17:23a, NKJV).

God created and blessed the union of a man with his wife. In it is a picture of something so holy, so intimate, it seems impossible to believe. The enemy has taken every opportunity to destroy our understanding of this joining. I believe he fears this revelation above all others; for when the people of God come to a true understanding of the oneness we share with Him, darkness will find no place in the earth.

Here is a picture of a woman through the eyes of her beloved. He describes her features in language that is strange, even puzzling to the western mind. Yet one thing is clear; he knows her intimately. The language leaves no doubt of that.

I have discovered something about God. He is not afraid of using sexual images to reveal spiritual truths. If God were averse to speaking in sexual images, why would He choose circumcision as the sign of His covenant with Abraham? Why does He speak of lovers, even unfaithful lovers, throughout the Scriptures to describe His relationship with mankind?

In a world where lust has colored and shaped our understanding of sexuality, finding the honor and purity of true sexuality is like discovering a perfect lily in the midst of a garbage heap. Such a lily is this passage.

The bridegroom's earlier description of the bride (Song 4:1-4) was a seven-fold picture from her head down. He now describes her beauty from her toes to her hair. He names thirteen attributes: her feet, thighs, navel, waist, breasts, neck, eyes, nose, head, hair, stature, breath, and mouth. Let us approach this passage with the heart to see the bride (and ourselves) through His eyes.

PRINCE'S DAUGHTER

"How beautiful are your feet in sandals,
O prince's daughter" (Song 7:1).

I wondered as I began to study this passage why the Lord began with the bride's feet. All of the other descriptions in the Song are from the head down. As I pondered this, the Lord reminded me that when He returns His feet will stand upon the Mount of Olives and all of the earth will come under His authority. Abraham was instructed to walk the length and breadth of the land for it belonged to him. Feet upon the land are a sign of possession.

Feet in sandals speak of readiness. Ephesians 6:15 tells us our feet are shod with the good news which is the message of peace. But there is also the aspect of identity. What did the prodigal's father give to him immediately upon his return? Shoes, a ring, and a robe - shoes.

The bride's shoes point to her identity - prince's daughter. One who was once an orphan - left without the protection, provision, and identity of a father - has been named a child of the king. She has come to know her father and walks in the shoes of his providing.

The bride now has access to her father. She was once an orphan, but her perception of herself is changing as she discovers the name and nature of the one who loves her. "Therefore My people shall know My name; therefore they shall know in that day that I Am He who speaks: Behold, it is I!" (Isaiah 52:6, NKJV).

Israel is the name God gave to Jacob, Prince with God. Prince's daughter identifies the bride as an heir to this promise. She is transformed as she walks in the identity her father has given her. Her sandals/identity are foundational to this transformation.

> "How beautiful are your feet" suggests another passage found
> in Isaiah: "How beautiful upon the mountains Are the feet of
> him who brings good news, Who proclaims peace, Who
> brings glad tidings of good things, Who proclaims salvation
> Who says, to Zion, 'Your God reigns!'" (Isaiah 52:7, NKJV).

I carry a picture in my spirit that when the bride moves the earth shakes. She stands in great authority and has learned to wield it by declaring the immutable truths of heaven. The earth shakes as if a giantess were moving across the land. She has become the Prince's daughter with beautiful feet in sandals because she understands this: Power belongs to God.

A JEWELED FOUNDATION

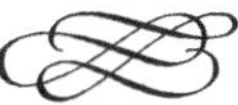

"The curves of your thighs are like jewels,
the work of the hands of a skillful workman" (Song 7:1).

Thighs are the foundation of the body. They are the strong muscles on which the body depends to stand upright and to walk.

A jeweled foundation is a picture found in several places in Scripture. In Isaiah 54, the Lord comforts His people with the words, "Your Maker is your Husband." He speaks of His bride as a city and says, "I will lay your stones with colorful gems and lay your foundations with sapphires" (Isaiah 54:1, NKJV).

The bride is seen in Revelation 21 as a city coming out of heaven filled with the glory of God; her light is like a precious stone, clear as crystal. The wall of the city has twelve foundations which are adorned with all kinds of precious stones. We are also told in this passage that upon the twelve foundations of the city are the names of the twelve apostles of the Lamb. Clearly, the stones represent people.

The Hebrew word for jewel is "segullah." It speaks of something which is closely guarded, a special treasure. In Exodus 19:4-5 (NKJV), God offers a passionate plea to His people with these words, "You have seen what I did to the Egyptians and *how* I bore you on eagles' wings and brought you to Myself. Now therefore, if you will indeed obey My voice and keep My covenant, then you shall be a special treasure to Me above all people; for all the earth *is* Mine."

Jesus said, "Again, the kingdom of heaven is like treasure hidden in a field, which a man found and hid; and for joy over it he goes and sells all that he has and buys that field" (Matthew 13:44, NKJV).

If you see the bride as the treasure hidden in the world, Father as the man who found her, and Jesus as the price He gave to buy the field, the puzzle of this parable falls into place.

The promise rests upon the covenant God made with His people. We find it in Genesis 17:7, "And I will establish My covenant between Me and you and your descendants after you in their generations, for an everlasting covenant, *to be God to you* and your descendants after you (NKJV, *emphasis mine*)."

If God is my God, I find my identity in Him. I am His jewel, His precious treasure. If God is my God, all is well. He is Almighty. I will give Him all my fear, because He alone is worthy to be feared.

The act of accepting our identity as God's treasure places us in a position of strength. We have strength to walk, strength to run, and strength to stand. We have become the habitation of God in the earth, and we carry His presence wherever we go. But how does this come about in our lives? Let us ponder for a moment the words, "the work of the hands of a skillful workman."

When Moses was given the instructions for the tabernacle, God said, "See, I have called by name Bezalel, and I have filled him with the Spirit of God, in wisdom, in understanding, in knowledge, and all manner of workmanship to design artistic works . . . in cutting jewels for setting . . . and to work in all manner of workmanship" (Exodus 31:2-5, NKJV).

The skillful workman was specifically called and purposely filled with artistic ability by the Holy Spirit. The artist's ability belonged first to God. God put it into a man, who then produced the beautiful pieces according to the plans which came from the mind of God.

God gave Bezalel wisdom to make beautiful designs which were never before seen upon the earth. They were the designs of heaven. Bezalel and those who worked with him brought into the view of mankind replicas of the things of heaven. The furnishings, garments, and ornamentations mirrored the originals which are eternal.

The Holy Spirit is at work in us to present us as flawless jewels in the presence of God. Jude 24 tells us God "is able . . . to present you *faultless* before the presence of His glory" (NKJV, *emphasis mine*). The Holy Spirit is the Skillful Workman shaping us into the design God intended when He first thought of us.

I know it seems somewhat fanciful to think of ourselves as jewels. Perhaps you are thinking, "Jewels are valuable and beautiful, and I'm just ordinary me."

Did you know jewels are made from ordinary elements? Diamonds, I am told, are formed when carbon is put under intense heat and pressure. I doubt there is a person reading this who would say they had never felt pain or pressure in their life. Hmm, maybe God could do something with an ordinary person like me.

I remember the day I saw Jesus standing before me holding a large, intricately cut diamond in His hand. The diamond was brilliant and multi-faceted, very beautiful. In the center of the diamond was a perfectly formed red rose, velvety and soft. My eyes were drawn irresistibly to the rose as the facets of the diamond revealed its delicate beauty in every plane. The rose was a living thing within the stone.

This is the way our lives display the beauty of God's life in us. God has entrusted to each one of us a unique revelation of Himself. I am the only me, and you are the only you. It is God's design in us that makes us special and unique. We are His jewels, and He is the rose inside. As we learn to agree with God for our own unique identity, more clarity comes into the facets of our souls and more of His beauty shines through.

WATER AND WINE

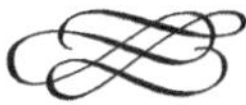

"Your navel is a rounded goblet;
it lacks no blended beverage" (Song 7:2).

The Hebrew word for navel is "shorer." The word translated goblet is "sahar." The bride's "shorer Sahar" lacks no "mezeg." "Mezeg" is tempered wine; a blend of water and wine.

Jesus spoke of a river of living water flowing from the belly of one who believes in Him. John stated the river was in reference to the Holy Spirit whom those who believe in Jesus would receive (John 7:37-39).

Wine is from the fruit of the vine. At Cana, Jesus turned the water contained in six stone pots into wine. Remember six is the number for man. At Jesus' directive, what was ordinary within the pots became extraordinary (John 2:1-11).

And Jesus spoke of putting new wine into new wineskins when He instructed His disciples about the changes required when people leave their former religion behind to enter into relationship with Him (Matthew 9:14-17).

In pondering these passages, it appeared to me that wine pictures the spirit of regenerate man; the spirit of one who is alive in God.

"Mezeg" is a blended beverage of water and wine together. Thanks to my eighth-grade science teacher, I understand that when you blend two like substances together, it forms a solution. A solution is different from a mixture in that when the two parts are mixed together, they form a new substance. A mixture could be separated for they never actually become one, like sand and pebbles or water and oil. But a solution is a new substance. The two parts together become one.

The navel is the center of our beings, the point at which we were once attached to our mothers and through which we received life-giving nourishment. The Holy Spirit is the Nurturer. He is the one who brooded over the formation of creation and who continues to brood over our lives until the character of Christ is fully formed in us.

"Your navel is a rounded goblet; it lacks no blended water and wine." Here is a picture of the inclusive heart of God. When we give our hearts to God, He gives His Spirit to us, then our spirit and His Spirit come together to become one.

The Holy Spirit is our Teacher and our Comforter. As He fills us, the very presence of God flows into us and through us. There is no lack of this beverage, no shortage, no need to jostle for position to "get mine." The Holy Spirit is a never-ending river of nurturing and refreshing to and through the bride.

There is a beautiful passage in Ezekiel which pictures the river flowing from the holy place. This river flows from the seat of God and gives life to all within its scope. "And it shall be *that* every living thing that moves, wherever the rivers go, will live. There will be a very great multitude of fish, because these waters go there, for they will be healed, and everything will live wherever the river goes" (Ezekiel 47:9, NKJV).

God has taken up residence within the bride. His life is joined to hers and now flows out through her as irresistibly as the water of a river flows forth from its source. Wherever the bride goes, she carries the river with her, and where the river goes there is life.

HARVEST IN REST

"Your waist is a heap of wheat set about with lilies" (Song 7:2).

Jesus likened wheat to people when He said, ". . . Lift up your eyes and look at the fields, for they are already white for harvest!" (John 4:35, NKJV).

And in another place He said, ". . . The harvest truly is plentiful, but the laborers are few. Therefore pray the Lord of the harvest to send out laborers into His harvest" (Matthew 9:37-38, NKJV).

Among the Old Testament sacrifices in Leviticus 23, we find a curious offering. At the beginning of harvest, Israel was instructed to cut a sheaf of wheat and offer it as a wave offering to the Lord. It was an offering of the first fruits of the harvest. Along with the sheaf of grain, they were instructed to offer an unblemished one-year-old male lamb as a burnt offering to the Lord. The burnt offering of the lamb caused the rest of the harvest to be received by God with the same degree of acceptance as the initial wave offering.

The Apostle Paul tells us Jesus is the first fruits and those who follow Him are the harvest (1 Corinthians 15:20-28). If the initial wave offering represents Jesus the Son of Man, and the harvest represents the rest of us; the image clearly shows the heart of Father toward us. He offers us the same degree of acceptance that He extends toward His Son.

As amazing as this is, it is taken a step further by the prayer Jesus prayed on the night He was betrayed. Jesus prayed for those who would come to believe in Him, and He said to His Father regarding us, "You . . . have loved them as You have loved Me" (John 17:23, NKJV, *paraphrased*).

"Your waist is a heap of wheat . . ." The bride's waist is likened to a heap of wheat indicating that her waist (or womb) is a place of fruit-fulness. The bride has within her the capacity to bring forth a harvest of souls; children born of the Spirit, the Lord's beloved offspring.

This harvest is "set about with lilies" which speaks of the rest we have entered into as the people of God. Lilies represent a quiet heart found in the contentment of living in the presence and provision of God.

The harvest is birthed through intimacy as the bride enters into the peace she finds in the loving acceptance of God.

IN ONE ACCORD

"Your two breasts are like two fawns, twins of a gazelle" (Song 7:3).

This is the third time this analogy has been given. Two breasts like two fawns, twins. The repetition of two said three ways three times indicates this is more than a mere feature of admiration to the bridegroom. The emphasis is far too marked to be passed over.

Breasts are a picture of the heart. The heart in this case is more than one; two, yet the same. At first, I thought it was merely a picture of loveliness and mystery. It is that, but this is a picture of the bride; many people coming together to form the whole. This is the bride of Christ; the church made perfect, prepared as a bride for her husband. Therefore, the emphasis of beautiful hearts which are two, yet identical, speaks of the people of God in unity. Here is a group of people who are committed to the Lord, and to one another.

On the night before He died, Jesus said, "This is My commandment, that you love one another as I have loved you. Greater love has no one than this, than to lay down one's life for friends" (John 15:12-13, NKJV).

On the Day of Pentecost following Jesus' resurrection, the disciples were "with one accord in one place" (Acts 2:1).

Loving one another and living in unity is seen in the gentleness of the two fawns, who share parentage – who even shared a womb; both equally cherished by the gazelle who bore them, neither needing to fight for a place of pre-eminence.

Learning to love one another as God loves us is something God deeply desires for us. Placing the desire of God for our unity above our differences will challenge our self-righteousness and our conceit. The love we offer may not be reciprocated, but it will bless the one who loves us.

We cannot answer for the way our brother responds to us, but we can determine within ourselves to offer to others the same unselfish love that our Father gives to us. This love is gentle, meek, peaceable, and does not keep a record of wrongs. The love God offers us has no strings and no qualifying demands.

The picture is of two, three times; two breasts, like two fawns, twins of a gazelle. Two speaks of agreement; but two three times is more than people coming together, it is the agreement of human hearts with God's.

Jesus offers His help to us as we lean into Him. He invites us to come to Him to trade our arrogance for His humility, and our self-satisfaction for His dependence upon His Father. He said, "Come to Me all you . . . heavy laden, and I will give you rest. Take My yoke upon you and learn of Me, for I am gentle and lowly in heart and you will find rest for your souls" (Matthew 11:28-29, NKJV).

When we fill our vision with Jesus and lean into Him, it becomes easy to say to our brother, "I've been shown far too much mercy to exact payment from you."

NOT MY WILL

"Your neck is like an ivory tower" (Song 7:4).

The aspect of the bride once seen as a tower David built for an armory upon which hung a thousand shields has become an ivory tower. The bridegroom's body is described as carved ivory. The bride's neck represents her will. That her neck is now seen as an ivory tower indicates the bride has joined herself to her bridegroom in his humility.

Jesus gave up His claim to pre-eminence and took the place of a servant, suffering and dying, while relying upon His Father for wisdom and strength in all that He did. Jesus said on several occasions He did only what He saw His Father doing. His reliance upon His Father was absolute.

In Paul's letter to the Philippians, he describes his claim to righteousness through the law. He met every requirement given to Moses. He was blameless according to the law in conduct and zeal. But when he met Jesus on the road to Damascus, all that had once been a treasure to him, all that had given him such surety of righteousness and confidence before God and man, he now saw as waste instead of gold. None of it mattered anymore. All he wanted afterwards was to know Jesus.

The bride has brought her will into conformity with God's will. She may not know everything He wants for her and from her, but she is determined to choose His will in favor of her own. The same trust and expectancy of resurrection life which was in the heart of Jesus as He uttered the words, "not My will, but Yours, be done" (Luke 22:42, NKJV), now resonates in her heart. She is beholding Jesus as the Author and Perfecter of her faith.

Scales have fallen from her eyes, and she sees what had been hidden from Adam's seed for six thousand years. The neck that held a thousand shields is now transformed into the likeness of the body which took the stripes and the nail and spear wounds for her sake.

Thousand is the number which speaks to me of holiness, as it is ten which is the number for righteousness or the good will of God to the third power, three – the number for the Godhead, the Trinity. Ten to the third power; the fullness of God's goodness: holiness. The bride knows holiness belongs to God. She has laid her will before the Lord in utter dependence upon Him, just as her Bridegroom did before her.

The devil stood apart from God and declared: "I will, I want, I won't," and Adam's race has followed him there. Now the bride has made the choice to stand with God. She is convinced of this truth: "the will of God is good and acceptable and perfect" (Romans 12:2, NKJV). She has determined there is nothing outside of the will of God which is worth more to her than the oneness she now shares with Him. Her neck is like an ivory tower.

Dear friend, I have determined in my heart before the Lord that I would share my journey with you whether it is pretty or not. Here is my story regarding having a neck of ivory and a heart as twins of a gazelle.

I love God very much, but I have seen much wrong done in the name of religion and have very little patience for what I see as bondage to legalism. Having said that, I will tell you that I know a man (he is a good-hearted man), who tries very hard to point everyone in his world toward salvation in Jesus. He uses every means at his disposal to "witness," often using shame and guilt to turn people's behavior in the direction he wants them to go.

One day I'd had enough and sent him an e-mail expressing my displeasure at his tactics, pointing out that God is loving and gentle, not harsh toward us. Ironic, isn't it? Well, as soon as the e-mail was sent, I felt the Lord ask me if what I had done was something He had asked of me. Um, no, I knew it wasn't. I was "helping." I knew I had overstepped, and the Lord was grieved.

There was no way to retract the e-mail and cover my mistake. This was something I was going to have to walk through to correct. As I prayed about what to say, my friend answered me with an apology for the offense he had caused. By now the pain I had caused the Lord by my arrogant act was throbbing in my heart. The Lord made me understand He is able to speak to His own servant, and I am not called to police the body of Christ.

I sent another e-mail apologizing for my arrogant words, for which I received a loving reply. Having done what I could to repair the damage with my friend, I went to the Lord with my broken heart and laid out before Him my arrogance, pride, and conceit. I was so focused on my wrong doing that, when He spoke in reply, I was speechless and could hardly take it in.

Fresh tears of sorrow at my unlikeness to Him now mixed with joy at His goodness toward me; for the words He spoke so clearly to my heart in that moment were, "Your neck is a tower of ivory."

I still find I am speechless at these words. I don't understand how such a wrong thing in me could be the means to prompt the Lord to give me such a commendation. Well, I do understand; it wasn't the arrogance that brought the commendation, but the repentance. Still, I know I am riddled with conceit. I am very likely to speak out without thinking again in just such a way. How can He say my neck is like ivory?

Even as I write this, I feel His gentle answer; He sees my heart is His, and my will is turned toward Him. So I conclude: a neck of ivory is found not in perfect behavior, but in a repentant heart whose will it is to seek after God.

FACING THE DAWN

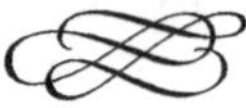

"Your eyes like the pools in Heshbon
by the gate of Bath Rabbim" (Song 7:4).

*E*yes are the windows of the soul. The bridegroom looks into the eyes of his bride and sees them as the clear pools of water by which weary travelers and their animals kneel to rest and find refreshment.

Heshbon was a city east of the Jordan. It was a city which greeted travelers coming out of the wilderness prior to crossing the river on their way up to Jerusalem. The Hebrew root for the word Heshbon means "to contrive, to think, conceive, consider." It is a word which speaks of intelligence and the ability to understand.

Bath Rabbim literally means "daughter of a multitude." Bath is the feminine word for offspring. Cities were often referred to in a feminine form, much in the way ships are spoken of as female. The word Rabbim is from a root which means "abundant, exceedingly full, plenteous, mighty, multiplied, and myriad."

The eyes of the bride have become quiet pools of deep understanding, filled with the vision of her beloved. She offers a welcome spring of life-giving water to the thirsty multitudes who come to her door.

"Your nose is like the tower of Lebanon
which looks toward Damascus" (Song 7:4).

Damascus is east of Lebanon, toward the rising sun. Sunrise marks a new day: hope, the passing of the night. Her face set toward Damascus suggests her heart is turned toward "He who arises with healing in His wings" (Malachi 4:2, NKJV).

The sunrise begins with a lightning sky. The darkness decreases. Black turns to grey. As the kaleidoscope turns another degree, purple becomes pink; pink turns to blue; then glorious gold bursts into view, revealing the face she most longs to see.

Keeping her face turned toward the sunrise is setting her will to wait for the dawn. She has learned her Sovereign is faithful. Whether in daylight or darkness, she maintains this vigilant posture. He is as faithful as the sunrise. She is resolute. Her face is turned always toward him as she watches and waits for his coming.

In Psalm 130:6 (NKJV) we read, "My soul waits for the Lord, more than those who watch for the morning – yes, more than those who watch for the morning."

THE LORD IS GOD

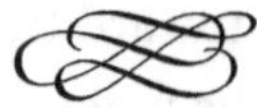

"Your head crowns you like Carmel" (Song 7:5).

Approximately eight hundred and seventy years before Jesus' birth, Ahab was king in Israel. He took as a wife a woman who was steeped in demon worship. Ahab and his wife taught the people of Israel to leave their worship of God. The people followed the example of the king as he learned the arts of Baal worship from Jezebel, his wife. The objective of the queen was to get all she could by way of manipulation and domination. Jezebel wanted control.

The worship of Baal was based on power and control. People were only important if they could further the designs of the king. The land was filled with violence. Human life was cheap. The people of Israel had forgotten their God. They had become like the world all around them – living to please themselves.

Into this teeming darkness God sent Elijah to say to the king, "There shall not be dew nor rain on the earth except at my word." Rain speaks of blessing. Dew is a sign of favor. The favor of God had been withdrawn. His blessing was withheld. It was a call for the people to turn back; a chance for them to remember their God.

The children of Israel were His covenant people. God had promised Abraham that his children would be God's family. Yet the children of Israel had turned from their God. They had forgotten His goodness and had begun to serve those who would destroy their lives.

The drought was severe. Rivers slowed to a trickle and then turned to dust. Crops failed. There came a famine in the land. Ahab convinced himself Elijah was responsible for the famine and the drought, so he sent couriers to search for him in every corner of the kingdom, but Elijah could not be found. Elijah was hidden away to the north of Israel on the Mediterranean coast.

Three years went by. Then God spoke to Elijah and said, "Go tell the king God will send rain on the earth once more." When Elijah arrived in Israel, Ahab's first words to him were, "Is that you, O troubler of Israel?" But Elijah answered, "I have not troubled Israel, but you in forsaking the commandments of our God and following the Baals."

Elijah then challenged the four hundred and fifty prophets of Baal and the four hundred prophets of Asherah to a contest to demonstrate who the true God is. Then the prophets of Baal along with many of the people of Israel gathered on the slopes of Mount Carmel.

When Elijah saw the people, he cried out, "How long will you falter between two opinions? If the Lord is God, follow Him; but if Baal, follow him." But the people did not answer.

The contest took place in this way: the four hundred and fifty prophets of Baal were to build an altar and lay a sacrificed bull upon it but put no fire under it. They would then call upon their gods to send fire to consume the sacrifice. Elijah would also prepare an altar and a bull. They all agreed that the God who answered by fire – is God.

So from early morning until the heat of the day, the prophets of Baal called upon their gods. They danced and shouted and cut themselves until the blood ran from their bodies, but there was no fire under the sacrifice. Not even a whiff of smoke.

Then Elijah called the people to come near to him. He repaired the altar of the Lord that had been broken down, and added to the altar twelve stones - one to represent each of the tribes of Israel - declaring as he did so, "Israel shall be your name."

The Scripture says, Elijah took the twelve stones and built an altar in the name of the Lord. He dug a trench around it, put wood on the stones, and laid the bull upon it. Then he had twelve pots of water poured over the altar until water ran all around the altar. He also filled the trench with water.

When everything was ready, Elijah prayed, "Lord God of Abraham, Isaac and Israel, let it be known this day that You are God in Israel, and that I, Your servant, have done these things at Your word. Hear me, O Lord, hear me, that this people may know that You are the Lord God, and that You have turned their hearts back to You again."

Immediately the fire of the Lord fell and consumed the burnt sacrifice, the wood, the stones, the dust, and all of the water in the trench. When the people saw it, they fell on their faces and said, "The Lord, He is God! The Lord, He is God!"

Then Elijah said to them, "Seize the prophets of Baal! Do not let one of them escape!" So they seized them; and Elijah brought them down to the Brook Kishon and executed them there. (1 Kings 18, *paraphrased*)

The bride's head crowns her like Mount Carmel; the place where the people understood and confessed, "The Lord is God." The mind of the bride is settled on this point: The Lord is God. She will neither worship nor fear any other. Her crown is more than ornamentation. It is a victor's crown.

She has waged the battle over her mind and has entered into agreement with Paul's declaration in 2 Corinthians 10:3-5 (NKJV), "For though we walk in the flesh, we do not war according to the flesh. For the weapons of our warfare are not carnal but mighty in God for pulling down strongholds, casting down arguments and every high thing that exalts itself against the knowledge of God, bringing every thought into captivity to the obedience of Christ."

Regardless of the political climate or the popular beliefs of the culture in which she lives, the bride stands before the perpetrators of darkness (the prophets of Baal) and declares, "The Lord is God." She knows her name is Israel, prince's daughter, and her identity with the Lord who is God gives her both the authority and strength to stand.

PURPLE HAIR

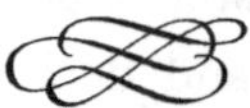

"And the hair of your head is like purple,
a king is held captive by your tresses" (Song 7:5).

The hair of the bride's head is a metaphor for what grows out of or extends from her head – her thoughts. It describes her tresses as purple and says a king (or royal) is held, yoked, or girded in them. It is clearly a description of the bride's royal perspective. She has been "transformed by the renewing of her mind" (Romans 12:2) and has entered heaven's view of life.

Jesus' life and teachings were a presentation and demonstration of the kingdom of heaven. The life He calls us to live in this world is as a citizen of His kingdom, following Him in the heart and power of kingdom living.

What are the marks of a heavenly royal? Jesus said, "By this all will know that you are My disciples, if you love one another" (John 13:35, NIV).

Love is the foremost mark of a royal of heaven. Love is more than kindness, more than gentleness. Love is ferocious in battle over the well-being of a loved one. Love seeks and calls for the highest and best in the other.

The bride has learned to comfort where true comfort is needed, but does not allow herself to be manipulated by selfishness. She seeks the well-being of her loved one and has learned to walk uprightly; not bending toward brokenness in others, but instead causing them to learn to stand upright as well. "Love does not rejoice in iniquity (crookedness) but rejoices in the truth" (1 Corinthians 13:6, NKJV).

Love has staying power, committing itself to a loved one in an unbreakable bond. Love seeks what is best for the sake of the loved one and does not draw back in the face of challenges and difficulties.

The little poem, "Outwitted," by Edwin Markham, says it this way, "He drew a circle to keep me out, heretic, rebel, a thing to flout, but Love and I had the wit to win, we drew a circle that took him in."[1]

Love believes in the loved one; believing in the image God holds of them, not allowing mistakes or lesser behaviors to shadow that image in her mind. The bride's love calls the heart of her loved one into agreement with the goodness of God. She declares the true image of God over her loved one, until that one comes into the fullness of that truth. Love speaks what God is saying concerning her loved ones, taking His word as the true assessment of their lives, thereby giving strength to what is good and calling them into freedom.

Love is respectful and honoring. The bride sees the people around her through the eyes of her Lord. She offers the same love she has been so freely given to these others who are also beloved of God. This love extends beyond emotional needs into the tangible realm, leading her to offer what she has to meet what needs she can.

The purple hair of the bride is a picture of kingdom-mindedness streaming from the head of the bride. Her head crowns her with the declaration "the Lord is God," and out of that established fact she lives as a royal of heaven upon the earth. Love is the hallmark of her life, and life flows wherever she goes.

HABITATION

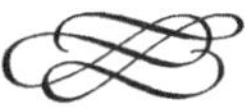

The bridegroom then says, "How fair and how pleasant you are, O love, with your delights! This stature of yours is like a palm tree, and your breasts like its clusters. I said, 'I will go up to the palm tree, I will take hold of its branches'" (Song 7:6-8).

He likens her stature to a tree which is recognized the world over as being straight and tall. It is an idiom for her character. Her stature is as upright as a palm. Among the meanings of the root word for stature are: to endure, help, lift up, remain, strengthen, succeed, and uphold.

The clusters of the palm tree refer to the sweet and juicy dates, which are both refreshing and satisfying. Date palms are a welcome sight in an oasis, providing the traveler with both food and shade.

Jesus said, "Of the abundance of the heart the mouth speaks" and "by their fruit you shall know them" (Luke 6:44-45, NKJV). The breasts of the bride are likened to the nutritious and sustaining fruit of this tree. What a lovely analogy for the life-giving words which come forth from her heart.

The bridegroom says, "I will go up to the palm tree, I will take hold of its branches." In Leviticus 23, the children of Israel were given instructions concerning the feast of booths. They were told to take palm branches and build shelters to stay in for the duration of the feast, and then to rejoice before the Lord their God. The booths symbolized the time the people left Egypt and found their shelter in the Lord their God. The feast of booths was a celebration that pointed to the day when the bride would be the dwelling of God, and God would be found in her.

We also find palm trees, along with cherubim and flowers, carved on all of the walls of the sanctuary of the temple (1 Kings 6). This is another place where we can see the temple as the hearts of people. It is God's preferred dwelling place.

The branches of the palm tree signify the victory of our redemption. Revelation 7:9-17 speaks of the great multitude from every nation standing before the throne of the Lamb, with palm branches in their hands and crying out with a loud voice, "Salvation belongs to our God who sits on the throne, and to the Lamb!" The passage goes on to describe the worship before the throne, and then says, "He who sits on the throne will dwell among them" (*paraphrased*).

The fear of death, the oppression and control of worldly things, have lost their power over the bride. She is safe in her God. She no longer has to protect herself from evil. He who is in her is the greater one. She is more than a conqueror through Him who loves her.

Palm branches represent a dwelling place of God among men. Before He went to the cross Jesus told His disciples that He would ask the Father to send the Holy Spirit to live inside of us. He said He is "the Spirit of truth, whom the world cannot receive, because it neither sees Him nor knows Him; but you know Him, for He dwells with you and will be in you" (John 14:17, NKJV).

Seeing the bride as a palm tree recognizes that God has come to make His home in her.

TOGETHER IN UNITY

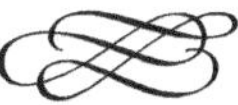

"Let now your breasts be like clusters of the vine" (Song 7:8).

n John 15:1-17, Jesus describes the relationship of the branch to the vine and of the vine to the husbandman. He instructs us that in order for there to be life in us, we must "abide" in Him; that is, we must live in unbroken communion with Him. Jesus makes it clear it is not only possible, it is expected that our lives are to be lived in continuous fellowship with God.

Jesus explains it is within this place of abiding that we will experience the fullness of His love, and the joy which is constant there. Unbroken fellowship is the result of living in agreement with the Father. The relationship Adam had with God in Eden has been restored to the people who abide in the vine. Jesus explains He has taken us from a place of mere servanthood into friendship with Him, for He shares His secrets with us and makes known His Father's plans.

All of this is illustrated as a branch living in the vine. The supply of life in God satisfies our needs. When life overwhelms us, He lifts and carries us. When we experience fruitfulness, He increases our capacity to become even more fruitful.

But the bridegroom says, "Let now your breasts be like clusters of the vine." He is calling his bride into an experience she hasn't previously known. Again, I believe the bride's breasts are referring to her heart.

Twice in this passage he pictures her breasts as clusters – first dates and now grapes. While I may not be very familiar with a cluster of dates, I do know how grapes grow on the vine. They hang together. They touch one another. They share a common source of nutrition. They experience the same sunlight and starlight. They are individual, yet are held in a common bond. They are the fruit of the vine and draw their life from it.

When Jesus gave the picture of abiding in the vine as a likeness for living in the love of God, He also commanded that we love one another. He even went so far as to say the love He commanded us to have for one another is to be as unselfish as His own love is for us – a love which is willing to lay down its life for another.

The bride's breasts, represented as clusters of the vine, are a picture of the hearts of individual people who are joined by the life they draw from the vine, living in selfless fellowship with one another.

The joining of hearts in the love of God is a source of absolute joy to our God. "How good and pleasant it is when brothers live together in unity!" (Psalm 133:1, NIV). I hear in this a cry from God's own heart.

It is both a command and a plea that we dwell together in unity. It is the place of commanded blessing where God is able to pour out His fullness upon His beloved.

As I prayed about these things one day not long ago, the Lord spoke these words to my heart, "Here is something I wish for you to understand. What I desire to give to you cannot be given to each alone. It is too big for you, as was the catch of fish Peter and John could not pull in and the boat could not contain" (Luke 5:4-10, NKJV).

"This is My desire for you, that you join your hearts together for My sake. That for love of Me you forgive one another, help one another, care for one another. The church of your city is your body. A body which hates itself, self-destructs." (I felt great pain in God's heart as He said this). "Turn away, therefore, from competition, self-consequence, suspicion, and rigidity. Make room for one another in your hearts. Pray for one another and pray with one another until your hearts burn together with the same holy fire of My love.

"I look for oneness among you that I may come to you with My weighty glory. Oneness is not sameness, however. Oneness comes when you have joined your hearts to Mine and given yourselves to Me in such abandon that love for Me is your nearest thought. Then the love which is in Me will fill and flow through you, supplying grace to you. My presence will flow through you like the continuous flow of a river, touching and transforming everything wherever you go with the eternal life which is in Me."

What God is asking of us is difficult because what is required in order to move into this river of the power and presence of God is costly to our souls. It will take a deep hunger, perhaps even desperation for the presence of God before we will be willing to give what it takes to go after the unity of the body.

I believe there is a day coming when the cry for this level of unity will become the echo resounding from every hill and valley where those who are the true bride worship. We will want the presence of God not just in our personal relationships with Him, but in the corporate expression to such an extent that we will be willing to do whatever it takes to enter this place of the commanded blessing. If this resonates with you, will you agree with me in this prayer?

Father, you said that You know the plans you have for us, plans to prosper and not to harm us, plans to give to us a future and a hope. I thank you, Holy Father. I don't yet know what this will be, but I trust your heart for me and for your church. I commit myself to do whatever you tell me to do to further the unity of the body. Transparency, vulnerability, humility – this is what you are looking for from us. You want our hearts uncovered so you can be our glory.

Adam and Eve were clothed in your glory. When the glory was gone, shame caused them to hide and cover themselves; but you shed blood to cover them once again. We are the same today. We try to protect our hearts with walls, silence, even anger. We resist vulnerability and refuse transparency, but transparency is the only way we can have your glory. Adam and Eve had to give up their fig leaves in order to receive the sacrificed lamb's skin.

Father, the enemy knows the power of unity. Division, fear, mistrust, confusion, misunderstanding, and so much besides swirl around us in the atmosphere. Father, I ask you for grace, great grace upon your church. Holy Spirit, please surround us and fill us. Help us to speak your words, choose your way, and seek your goodness to the praise and the honor of Jesus, whose blood was shed to restore your glory to those you love.

BREATHE IN, BREATHE OUT

"The fragrance of your breath is like apples" (Song 7:8).

Early in the Song, the bride describes the bridegroom as being like an apple tree among the trees of the wood. She sat down in his shade and his fruit was sweet to her taste. Two verses later, she implores him to refresh her with apples, for she is weak with love. It isn't difficult to find the source of the fragrance on the bride's breath.

Breath from the beginning has been a picture of the spirit of both God and man. God breathed into man "the breath of life" when He first formed him out of the dust of the earth, "and man became a living being" (Genesis 2:7).

Jesus breathed on His disciples following His resurrection in John 20:22 and said, "Receive the Holy Spirit." Then, to further affirm that it was the Spirit of God who was coming into them, He gave instructions to them regarding the forgiveness of sins.

In this illustration, the bride is filled with the love of her bridegroom to the degree that his scent is now within her. By this we understand that when the bride of Christ has been filled with the Holy Spirit, she receives resurrection life into her being.

Jesus gave His disciples the authority to speak and act in His stead. The bride also moves in His authority by the Spirit of God who is in her.

In Ezekiel 37, the prophet relates an experience he had with the Spirit of God. He saw a valley of bones. The bones were scattered and dry. The Spirit asked Ezekiel if the bones could live, and Ezekiel answered, "Oh Lord, You know." Then the Spirit of God directed Ezekiel to prophesy to the bones, speaking what was in God's heart regarding them.

So, in stages directed by the Holy Spirit, Ezekiel spoke the word of the Lord to the bones, prophesying and imparting until the bones came together with flesh upon them, and life in their beings. The final thing Ezekiel prophesied into the people who now stood before him as a great army was heart. Through the leading of the Holy Spirit, Ezekiel spoke hope and vision into the people, placing before them the will of God regarding their lives, and filling them with courage.

In this passage of the Song, we find the scent of apples on the breath of the bride. She is filled with the Spirit of God; so when she breathes, the atmosphere of God surrounds her, and when she speaks, she gives voice to the words He is speaking.

"The roof of your mouth is like the best wine" (Song 7:9).

Wine is seen as a blessing, a reason for rejoicing. The presence of wine is also an illustration of the human spirit that is alive to God.

The words which issue from the mouth of the bride originate in a palate given to blessing. The root for the "best wine" in this reference is a word meaning 'to effervesce.' There is a bubbling up quality, which could be seen as joy or liveliness. Interestingly, the Hebrew word "nabhi," translated "prophet," also carries with it the idea of one in whom a message from God bubbles up or springs forth.

Jesus turned water to wine at the wedding feast in Cana, and the description given of it was it was "the best wine." The bride's palate is like the best wine as she speaks life-giving words from the heart of God. But the joyous words of the bride are also toward her beloved. The wine she brings to Him is the worship which bubbles up and issues forth from her heart.

This is seen in the words which follow when the bride answers, "The wine goes down smoothly for my beloved, moving gently the lips of sleepers" (Song 7:9). The words "moving gently" or "gliding smoothly" can also mean "to cause to speak," and the word for "sleepers" can be translated "the ancient." So it could be seen as, "The wine goes down smoothly for my beloved, causing the ancient lips to speak."

I don't know which way is right, but I know when I worship and then quietly wait, I often hear the Ancient of Days speaking to my heart. It has been my experience that heartfelt worship brings an answering sound from heaven, like the sympathetic resonance from the strings of a finely tuned instrument when a harmonic is sounded nearby. Or perhaps, it is more true that the sound originates in heaven, and worship tunes our hearts to resonate with it.

There is one thing I noticed which I believe is important to point out in reference to the bridegroom's description of the bride: he doesn't mention her hands.

By contrast, the bride spoke gratefully of her bridegroom's hands as rods of gold (the hinges to the door of the holy place) covered in jewels. But as complete as the bridegroom's description is of his bride, there is no reference to her hands. His emphasis seems to be more about her stance as one of heaven's royals in the earth, her understanding of her identity, her heart given to love, and her words given to truth. He speaks of the fruitfulness of her being, but it isn't in reference to her work.

She stands; she loves; she blesses and worships; she believes; and in all of this she prospers; but it all comes from the oneness she shares with her bridegroom. His are the hands mentioned in the Song which embrace the bride and hold open the way into the holy place. The bride speaks of her bridegroom's hands, while his thoughts are with the heart of his bride.

KNOWING

"I am my beloved's, and his desire is toward me" (Song 7:10).

The great love of her bridegroom has found its way into every dark corner, uncovering every hidden shame, in the heart of the bride. The terror of his eventual rejection has gradually receded as each sinful act was revealed to the light, and she continued to find acceptance in his eyes. His love for her never faltered in the unveiling; no matter how deep the failing, nor how dark the wrong. The bride now stands in utter transparency before her beloved. She is wholly unafraid because she is absolutely assured of his love.

This verse for me is the centerpiece of the Song. It is the search light I have used upon my heart to find the broken foundations and hidden darkness there. It is the place in Him I saw long ago was mine to claim, yet for so many years could not occupy. Still, knowing it was there to have, was the promise which drew me in and took me on in my quest to know the heart of God for me.

This is the third time the bride makes a similar declaration. The first time, she said, "My beloved is mine, and I am his," giving her claim upon him the greater importance. The second time, she said, "I am my beloved's and he is mine." She had learned by then to place his claim upon her before her own. This time, however, there is no mention of her claim upon him. She has come to rest in a place where she knows she is loved, and his love is all to her.

"I am my beloved's and his desire is toward me." The word for desire in Hebrew is "teshuqa," and in both other places it is used, it is translated "turning." I like to think of this phrase, then, as "His heart is turned toward me," or sometimes I translate the verse, "I am His and His heart is wrapped around me."

I first found this verse at the beginning of my walk with the Lord, and immediately knew it was my home. There may be a verse of Scripture that you know, if you can only learn to dwell in it, your life will become what it was meant to be; this is that verse for me. But as much as I wanted to live out of this truth, it has taken a long time and a lot of determination to press through the fears and broken places in my heart to be able to say I have come to rest here. I knew God loved me in my head. It was in my heart that I struggled to believe.

It became my goal to say these words to my heart without quailing inside. I would often put this verse before my heart and use it to discover where I felt I had to push the words away. Then I would go to work on that place, asking the Lord to heal the hurt and teach me the truth. You see, I *knew* this was my rightful home; and they were only lies which were keeping me from it. The lies imprisoned me in fear; but often when I came to understand the lie which had hindered me, I was surprised at how tiny the twists were which had filled my world with turmoil.

Understanding came in stages, but the biggest breakthrough came the day I discovered Father has always loved me. He has always been near me to protect and care for me. It is so strange how one can believe a thing all of one's life, and yet not know it. Learning the truth about

God's love for us is the crux of the battle for liberty in our souls. It is often painful and difficult, but it is a battle worth fighting - that I promise you.

Like a tree planted in a fruitful place where the rich soil supplies all it needs to grow and flourish, causing it to become tall and strong so it can offer shade and bring forth fruit for others, making my home in these words which have established me in the heart of God has given me the freedom to become who I have always been meant to be. Knowing this truth, literally battling through until I believed it to the very depths of my being, has given me life. It has given me freedom, purpose, and strength until I have an overflowing abundance and can give life away.

I am His and He loves me. It is the beginning and the end, the totality of life.

It is God's heart's desire that we each learn to say, "I am His and He loves me. It is all I need. He is I Am. All of life is in Him. He has drawn me into Himself. As a child of my Father, I am loved, understood, cherished, protected, provided for, and even adored. I belong to Him, and He loves me.

Truly there is no better place. It is where I was always meant to be. It is where all that once pressed against me, all that caused distress, can no longer touch me. I have entered the secret place, the shadow of the Almighty, and nothing unworthy of Him can follow me there. I belong to Him and He loves me. It is all."

As I conclude the description of the bride through the eyes of her beloved, I would like to offer these words of encouragement. Perhaps you feel the image of this woman is far beyond you. I would like to remind you that what He looks for in you is willingness and desire. He does all of the rest. His are the hands.

One day, as I reviewed my journey into the knowledge of God, He spoke these words to my heart, "Walk with My, My child. You began to walk with Me many years ago. What a delight it has been for Me.

You remember struggles. I remember joys. Come with Me, My darling. Turn and see. Let Me bring your focus into agreement with the way I look at you. Let Me shift your focus from the darkness to the light. My grace I extend to you. My peace I give to you."

Your walk with God is His delight. Where you remember struggles, He remembers the joy of a heart wanting Him, choosing Him. He does not fault imperfection. He understands the process. He remembers our frame and loves us oh so tenderly. His enabling power is always present with us, and He freely gives us the well-being of His peace. There is nothing we lack which He does not supply. He formed us to be so filled by Him that our experience of a life shared with Him would be found even in the air we breathe.

ALL FOR YOU

"Come, my beloved, let us go forth to the field; let us lodge in the villages. Let us get up early to the vineyards; let us see if the vine has budded, whether the grape blossoms are open, and the pomegranates are in bloom. There I will give you my love. The mandrakes give off a fragrance, and at our gates are pleasant fruits, all manner; new and old, which I have laid up for you, my beloved" (Song 7:11-13).

Convinced she is accepted and loved, the bride now speaks out of joy in the freedom of her bridegroom's love. "Come, my beloved," she says, "Let us go forth to field and village and vineyard. Let us explore every corner of the kingdom of my heart. Let us pursue life in every part and put to rest every dark and hurtful thing. Let every doorway in my heart be a doorway for the life which is born in love. Let us search and see what fruit can be found there for you."

"The mandrakes give off a fragrance . . ." Mandrakes are an herb which was used as an aphrodisiac. Love surrounds the couple. It is even in the air.

"At our gates are pleasant fruits, all manner; new and old." She says, "I bring all of my life to this moment. I offer you access to everything in me for all that's within me is here to love you."

The bride has moved into the deep, flinging off all reserve, turning her heart and soul, will and strength, toward loving the one who loves her. He is worthy of her love and devotion. She may still be aware of her shortcomings, but they are on the periphery of her thoughts, for the fire that burns in her takes precedence over her weaknesses and failures. She can't be bothered with such inconsequential things. She recognizes that if He accepts her, then she must accept herself.

She turns her focus toward loving Him. Pouring out all that is within her as the fruit of her love, she offers her gifts of thanksgiving, trust, and a willing heart.

The bride's words sound in my heart like a prayer:

> *"Your love and acceptance have made me feel safe. Let us now search with all our heart. Please come with me and see what is growing there. In every orchard, field, and vineyard, let us look for the fruit of love.*

> *"I give all my heart and soul to you. I receive the promise of your fruitfulness for my life. I will not hold back out of shame, or fear of unworthiness. I will not draw back in unbelief. What you have begun in me, you will complete.*

> *"I am not afraid of any door in my heart. Every door is covered by your love. There is nothing in my history which cannot be redeemed. You are causing fruitfulness to blossom in my soul. Every memory, every shameful act, every hurtful thing, I now give to you as an offering of my love.*

> *"I trust your love for me. There is nothing I withhold from you. All my life: past, present, and to come – I offer to you, my Love. Your love*

has made me free to be vulnerable with you. Your love has given me life."

As I ponder these things, I find this prayer in my heart: "It is all for you, my Lord. Let us see what you can do in a heart wholly given to you. What can you bring forth from a life laid down? The blood of the Lamb is on the doorposts, and on the mercy seat of my heart. You have made my soul a sanctuary. Holy is the Lord, my God. You are I Am - present in my past, my present, and my future. Let all that I am, have been, or will become all that you can make of me."

CONSUMING PASSION

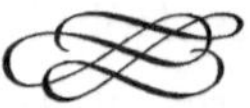

"Oh, that you were like my brother, who nursed at my mother's breasts! If I should find you outside, I would kiss you; I would not be despised. I would lead you and bring you into the house of my mother, she who used to instruct me. I would cause you to drink of spiced wine, of the juice of my pomegranate" (Song 8:1-2).

*I*t has become the bride's consuming passion to live in unbroken communion with her bridegroom; clean in heart and mind. She is wholly occupied with loving the person of her bridegroom. She waits every moment in joyful anticipation for his expressed will. He does not fail her, but extends his hand, inviting her to join him in the dance.

"Oh," she says, "Let us go! I want to share this joy with the people I love. I want them to know how happy your love has made me. I want to honor you before them. Before them I will make known my commitment to give to you all that my life can be – the juice of my pomegranate containing every promise of my life."

But mingled with her joy, there is sorrow; for the relationship she now has with her bridegroom is not welcome to those who were her former teachers. They do not welcome this display of passion. They prefer a more distant view of him, a more staid position. The bride's exuberance makes them uncomfortable. These who had been her teachers now try to talk her out of becoming too extreme. When she does not heed them and draw back from following him, they turn her away.

Her teacher's response to her beloved doesn't change her relationship with him. She long ago let go of her veils and came out from behind her locked door; but oh, that they would embrace him, and see him as she sees him. She finds herself despised, unheard, counted as insignificant among them; as one without a voice, or with a message of no worth.

Suffering the pain of rejection by those who had been her family, she turns to her bridegroom and says, "I wish those in the house of my mother understood the passion in my heart. They would permit the love I feel for you if I treated you as a brother. If you were like a brother to me, I could kiss you and bring you with me into the house of my mother and no one would look down on me. Then I could pour out all that is in my heart to you there. But here I am. I come to you. I lay my heart before you. I will be still in your arms."

> "His left hand is under my head,
> and his right hand embraces me" (Song 8:3).

His left hand under her head causes her to forget the pain of the rejection of those whose approval was once so important to her. The secret place of his presence is all she wishes for. If transparency before others is what he asks of her, she offers it as a gift of her love. It is the least she can do. His right hand embraces her, filling her with the promise of her fulfilled destiny.

With the words, "I charge you, O daughters of Jerusalem, do not stir up nor awaken love until it pleases" (Song 8:4), the bride says to those who watch and rejoice in her, "This love is requiring all I have to give. This love is taking me beyond myself. Whatever it asks of me, I cannot deny."

I also sense the bridegroom saying, "Let her rest. Allow her to remain in my arms. Do not try to pull her out of this place or make any demands upon her until she is ready."

In my own heart, I come to this passage and find a harmonic resonating within me at the sound of my Lord's heartbeat. He has given all to me. He suffered the loss of everything for the love of me. He was stripped, mocked, beaten, brutally treated, and hung on a cross to die as a criminal. He did it all for love of me, for love of you. He loves us more than the pain, more than the indignity, more than the horror of facing hell. He loves us more than misunderstanding and betrayal, more than being hated and reviled.

It is not shame. It is not guilt. Nor is it a sense of duty which causes my heartstrings to quiver as I ponder His love. I wait. I weep. I sigh, until the words rise up to express the sound of this song which is growing ever stronger within me.

> "Lord Jesus, I love you more! I love you more than my personal comfort, more than people's high opinion of me. I love you more, God! I will stand where you place me and speak what you give me to say. I will be vulnerable for your sake and trust in your right hand to keep me. You hide me in the secret place of your presence. I will be found under the shadow of the Almighty. Your heart is my home. Your glory is my covering. It is all. You are all."

PART VI

SONG OF SOLOMON 8:5-14, NKJV

Who is this coming up from the wilderness,
Leaning upon her beloved?

I awakened you under the apple tree,
There your mother brought you forth;
There she who bore you brought you forth.

Set me as a seal upon your heart,
As a seal upon your arm;
For love is as strong as death,
Jealousy as cruel as the grave;
It's flames are flames of fire,
A most vehement flame.
Many waters cannot quench love,
Nor can the floods drown it.
If a man would give for love
All the wealth of his house,
It would be utterly despised.

We have a little sister,
And she has no breasts.
What shall we do for our sister
In the day when she is spoken for?

If she is a wall,
We will build upon her
A battlement of silver;

And if she is door,
We will enclose her
With boards of cedar.

I am a wall,
And my breasts like towers;
Then I became in his eyes
As one who found peace.
Solomon had a vineyard at Baal Hamon;
He leased the vineyard to keepers;
Everyone was to bring for its fruit
A thousand silver coins.

My own vineyard is before me.
You, O Solomon, may have a thousand,
And those who tend its fruit two hundred.

You who dwell in the gardens,
The companions listen for your voice –
Let me hear it!

Make haste, my beloved,
And be like a gazelle
Or a young stag
On the mountains of spices.

A ROD, A MAN, AND GOD

There once was a man who wandered the rocky and arid land of the Arabian Peninsula tending a flock of sheep. He had been forty years in that place. His skin was leathery, and his body hardened by years of exposure to the elements. His self-confident dream of being an instrument of deliverance for his people was as faded as the garments he had worn upon his flight from Egypt. His beard and hair had grown long and turned grey. His image in the mirror held little to remind him of the cocky young man who used to walk the marble halls of Pharaoh's palace.

Occasionally, he felt a stirring in his heart that there was a greater purpose for his life; a noble purpose, a call to greatness; but he would push it away as an impossible dream. Still, like the flutter of a dry leaf lifted by a breeze, sometimes the stirring would arise unbidden and find its way into his consciousness as the whisper of a lullaby forgotten years before. He tried to keep a firm guard over these thoughts; for they were invariably accompanied by pain. But when the memories caught him unaware, a mocking voice would taunt him with the bitterness of his failure and lash him afresh with shame. He had failed. He had run. Murderer! Coward! Failure!

His mother must have been wrong. He was not the promised deliverer. God would have to find someone else; someone stronger, braver, wiser than he to carry out His plans. Moses had left Egypt knowing he could never go back. It was better to forget. But God does not forget.

Long before this day, God had made a promise to His friend, Abraham, saying Abraham's children would be afflicted in a foreign land, and at the end of four hundred years God would judge the people they served. God promised He would bring them out with great wealth and restore them to the land He had shown to Abraham.

As a child Moses had learned the story of his forefather, and the consciousness that he might be the means of deliverance was planted in his heart. The circumstances of his life pointed to that end: the miraculous preservation of his life in infancy, the training at his mother's knee, the privileges of his childhood being brought up as a son in Pharaoh's house, and the education and association with the most powerful men of his day. But on the day he attempted to fulfill the call, he ended by running for his life. Moses did not doubt the promise, only the chosen tool of deliverance.

Then one day while Moses rested on a sunbaked rock at the base of Mt. Horeb, as the sheep grazed nearby, he lifted his gaze and noticed in the distance a bush was burning. Curious, he drew closer; for though the fire did not spread, it continued to burn. How is this? The bush does not burn up.

Let us pick up the narrative as it unfolds in Exodus chapter three –

When the Lord saw that Moses drew near to see, He called to him from the midst of the bush, saying, "Moses, Moses!" And Moses answered, "Here I am."

Then God said, "Do not draw near this place. Take your sandals off your feet, for the place where you stand is holy ground. I am the God of you father – of Abraham, Isaac, and Jacob." At this Moses hid his face, for he was afraid to look upon God.

God continued, "I have surely seen the oppression of My people in Egypt and have heard their cry. I know their sorrows, so I have come down to deliver them out of the hand of the Egyptians and bring them up to a good and large land, a land flowing with milk and honey."

"Now therefore, behold, the cry of the children of Israel has come to Me, and I have seen the oppression with which the Egyptians oppress them. Come now, therefore, and I will send you to Pharaoh that you may bring My people, the children of Israel, out of Egypt."

I can imagine Moses' growing excitement as he listened to God relate His intention to at last bring deliverance to Israel. I feel sure he listened in amazement and with mounting joy - until God said, "Come, now therefore, I will send you."

Um, what? Remember me? I'm the one who tried and failed; I'm sure You can find someone better than me.

I think this accurately says what he felt when we see his answer to God. "Who am I that I should go to Pharaoh, and bring the children of Israel out of Egypt?"

God assured him, "I will certainly be with you, and when you bring the people out of Egypt you will worship Me on this mountain."

But Moses' experience with the children of Israel had taught him caution. The upbringing he had received as a son in the house of their oppressor caused him to appear as a traitor to his people, so he said, "When I come to the children of Israel and say to them, 'The God of your fathers has sent me to you,' and they ask me, 'What is His name?' What shall I answer them?"

Then God said to Moses, "I Am Who I Am. Thus, you shall say to them, I Am has sent me to you." Then, in detail, God laid out His plan to Moses of the deliverance of his people and where they were to go.

But Moses, still unconvinced God had made a good choice in His man for the job, questioned God again, saying, "What if they don't believe me, or listen to my voice? Suppose they say, 'God has not appeared to you.'"

So the Lord said to him, "What is that in your hand?" Moses said, "A rod." And God said, "Cast it on the ground." So, he cast it on the ground, and it became a serpent; and Moses fled from it. Then the Lord said, "Reach out your hand and take it by the tail." And he reached out his hand and caught it, and it became a rod in his hand.

There is much more to this story, but it encourages me to see how willing God was to give Moses the assurance he needed to return to Egypt in His name. Moses was certain he had been disqualified, but God had found in Moses precisely what He wanted.

Moses' early life was spent as the son of Pharaoh's daughter. In a sense, he grew up with a scepter in his hand. When he fled Pharaoh's court, he exchanged his scepter for a shepherd's rod. The rod was his constant companion. It was what he leaned upon when he was weary. It was both a weapon and tool. It became associated with his identity; for you can be sure he no longer thought of himself as an Egyptian prince. He had become a shepherd. So when he threw the rod down and it became a snake, it was an image of Moses' life. But at God's word to pick it up again, Moses took hold of the snake by its tail, and it became a rod once again. Yet with one great distinction; throughout the rest of Moses' story, whenever the rod is mentioned, it is called "the rod of God."

The rest of the story is well known to us. Moses went to Egypt and brought Israel out by many signs and miracles through the rod of God which he carried in his hand. Not divination, nor military power, nor the very elements of nature were able to stand before the power demonstrated by God as He set His people free.

When Moses threw the rod on the ground, it became the sign of a transfer of the ownership of his life. His life, what he could make of it, was represented in the snake slithering there. Moses had no illusions about his ability to deliver Israel. But at the word of God, Moses reached out and took the snake by the tail; just as by the bidding of God, he took hold of the purpose for his life once again.

It was not a golden scepter representing the honor due a ruler of Egypt. It was not even a shepherd's rod to give him a measure of comfort and security. It was a snake he reached out and took into his hand. He did not know when he picked up the snake if it would become a rod again; but in obedience to the voice of God, he did it. Obedience was what God was looking for in him.

Moses returned to Egypt after forty years in the wilderness. He went back at the bidding of God to finish the thing which in his own wisdom and strength he had attempted to do four decades before. He fully understood the Egyptian disdain for such as he had become. Shepherds were of the lowest strata of society. Returning with a rod in his hand would certainly not elevate him in their eyes. He did not return to Egypt in the power of his own wisdom, personal abilities, or strength. He returned simply as a man with a shepherd's rod in his hand.

But Moses had made an exchange that day at the base of Mt. Horeb. When he entered Pharaoh's court carrying his shepherd's rod, he knew it had become the rod of God. More than that, Moses knew, even as he held the rod in his hand, God held Moses in His.

WILDERNESS LESSONS

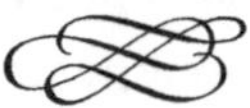

One day (I remember it like yesterday, although it seems a lifetime ago), I saw Jesus in a vision. He was standing before me with His hand outstretched in invitation. A few moments before, He had said to me, "I am going to deliver My people from darkness." And I had asked, "May come with You?"

He made me understand it would be difficult and painful for me, so I asked Him, "Will You be there to help me? Will I find You in that place?"

He let me know He would always be near me; every place I was to go He would take me. So I prayed, "Lord, please take me with You." Then, with the most beautiful light in His eyes, He stretched His hand out to me. When I laid my hand in His, I knew my life was about to change.

Life rarely looks the way we envision it. This experience was no exception. I did not know when I slipped my hand into His that it was the beginning of a wilderness season during which I would experience a shattering illness, the loss of a beloved parent, and painful changes in many other areas of my life. Also during this time, for a prolonged season, the tangible presence of the Lord which I had enjoyed as a constant refreshing stream receded to the point I felt I had to drill a well beyond bedrock nearly to the planet's core in order to find even a trickle of the water of the Holy Spirit.

I do not mean to imply there was no joy in my life. Along with my mother and much of the family, I was beside my dad when he entered heaven. I will never forget the look of wonder and amazement in his eyes as he looked beyond the ceiling and exhaled for the last time. We wept to see him go, but there is joy in the certainty we will join him there when our races have been run.

More than ever before, I feel I have a vested interest in heaven. The Lord has promised to comfort those who grieve. I have tasted the comfort of the Lord and have confidence that in His mercy there is all that is needed to heal the brokenhearted.

Illness taught me to live in the rest of God as nothing else could have done. It was necessary for me to stay in His rest. I had no physical or emotional strength to do my life apart from Him. Day by day as I struggled toward health, I learned to turn every worry and fear over to God, entrusting to Him all the weight of my life.

Isaiah 57:15 tells us, God dwells with the "contrite of heart." Contrite can also be translated as "powdered." I felt powdered, but I found a quietness of heart in God that became the peace which kept me through the days of weakness and pain. I thank God He gave me such a gift.

I think more than the grief and loss, more than the humiliating physical weakness, the hardest thing for me to endure in my wilderness was the dryness in my spirit – the loss of the sense of the nearness of God. But even this is something I am ever so grateful for.

During that time, I wanted Him so much I would sit for several hours each morning; listening, waiting, pondering the Scriptures until I found a drop of His life-giving dew. Then, when I had gained all I could find to sustain me, I would get up and do my day. From this experience, I learned to listen as I had never listened before.

Life does not look as we envision it, but God does not deceive us. Everything He promised He has done. I cannot reproach Him. My wilderness is all He said it would be. In it I learned the value of a life laid down.

In Hosea 2 the Lord describes what He does for His bride in the wilderness. We think of the wilderness as a desert place, but God promises it is where great fruitfulness will begin in her life. He says in the valley of troubling she will find a doorway of hope. There her childlikeness will be restored as she learns to come to Him in simplicity. He says she will learn to know Him as her husband and will no longer call Him "master." He promises His protection and provision. He promises the marriage between them will be filled with His love and mercy. She will rest in the safety of His justice, and in the peace of His righteousness. Throughout her time in the wilderness, she will experience His inescapable faithfulness, and will learn to trust in His goodness and power.

It is true. It is all true, just as Moses found. God meets His beloved in the wilderness. It is in the wilderness that God teaches us who we are – and who He is to us. Moses asked God, "Who am I?" and God answered, "I Am." It was his life laid down that positioned Moses to deliver Israel. He was no longer his own. His life was held in the hand of God.

AN UNVEILED MYSTERY

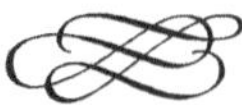

For the second time in the narrative, we find the bride emerging from the wilderness. The first time, she came seated in the palanquin surrounded by a military escort. She came out of the wilderness then as a royal bride, honored and protected, the choice of her king. At that time, she still had much to learn about being a wife. She was dazzled by the position she had been given. She was just beginning to discover the power at her husband's command. She had yet to understand his deep and unchanging love for her. Her love, then, still found much of its basis in performance as she measured her worthiness for his acceptance by her own behavior.

This time there is no pomp, no military escort. This time the couple comes walking out of the wilderness with their arms wrapped around one another and their bodies pressed close.

The daughters of Jerusalem ask, "Who is this coming up from the wilderness leaning on her beloved?" (Song 8:5). They are surprised by the bride's appearance. Something has changed in her.

But she does not seem to hear, and her bridegroom does not turn his eyes from her as he answers, "I awakened you under the apple tree.

There your mother brought you forth; there she who bore you brought you forth" (Song 8:5).With His eyes fixed on His bride, the King unveils the mystery of her identity with these words. "Under the apple tree I awakened you . . ."

"Before time began, I knew you. I saw you as you are now when I first formed man from the dust of the ground. I loved you in the beginning of creation, and breathed life into you then. I loved you in your infancy when you were helpless and despised. I loved you when you stumbled, when you strayed, and when you fell. I have never ceased to love you.

"Through all the long years of your wanderings, you did not know it then, but you were not alone. I have never left you. And now I have awakened you from the slumber of the ages. You are the issue of the faith of those who believed; the culmination of the promise Eve received. As in the beginning My breath gave you life, so now the fruit of My love in you is life forever more."

The bride, fully awake now, sees the hand that cared for her and brought her to this day. With wonder, gratitude, and every ounce of love in her being, she answers, "It is you. It's all you. It has only ever been you. You are the one who carried me; the one who stood as my advocate when I was condemned. You are the one who drew me back from despair and taught me to hope when all hope was lost. You are the one who paid the price, and it cost you all that you had."

She says, "Set me as a seal upon your heart, as a seal upon your arm; for love is as strong as death, jealousy as cruel as the grave; its flames are flames of fire, a most vehement flame" (Song 8:6).

The bridegroom answers, "Many waters cannot quench love, nor can the floods drown it. If a man would give for love all the wealth of his house, it would be utterly despised" (Song 8:7).

Or in other words, "It was not too much to give. Do you now under-stand your value? Do you see that all the wealth of My kingdom is nothing to Me compared to the exquisite joy I feel when you are with Me?"

Dear friend, do you see in the imagery the meaning I have found? Each phrase is rich and measureless, inviting us to explore the width and length, the depth and height, of the love of God; even as Paul prayed we would know the love that passes knowledge and be filled with the fullness of God (Ephesians 3:18-19).

Let us pause here for a moment and look more closely at the images given in this passage: "Under the apple tree, I awakened you."

Not long before this, the bride described her bridegroom as an apple tree. Under his shade, she found rest and his fruit was sweet to her taste. But let us pan back from the scene of the bride and her love to a garden long before, to a time when the mists of creation were just beginning to reveal the masterpiece which had been created in the heart of God.

There in the garden, God formed a bride as He drew her from the side of the man. She first came to awareness in His presence as she lay in the soft grass beneath the trees. In that garden was a tree called The Tree of Life. Jesus later said, "I am the life." Our bridegroom is the tree, the Source of Life. "There your mother brought you forth. There she who bore you brought you forth."

Immediately following the disobedience which gave darkness entrance into the world, God spoke to Adam and his wife and explained the heartbreaking consequences this would bring. He described their toil and their tears, but He also gave them a promise that through the seed of the woman would come the deliverer who would destroy forever the evil which had entered creation that day. With this promise, Adam honored his wife as the one who carried the hope of his salvation.

> "And Adam called his wife's name Eve,
> because she was the mother of all living" (Genesis 3:20, NIV).

Adam and Eve understood that breathing is merely existing, but life is found in fellowship with God. Eve's faith gave place to hope that life would return to Adam's race. She came into being under the Tree of Life and is mother to all who enter life through faith in the Promised One.

THE FLAME OF YAH

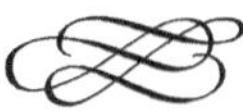

"Set me as a seal upon your heart, as a seal upon your arm;
for love is as strong as death, jealousy as cruel as the grave;
its flames are flames of fire, a most vehement flame" (Song 8:6).

Infinite God, within whose being all creation is contained, has in this passage given us a glimpse into the justice and mercy of heaven.

The seal is a signet; a stone engraved with a mark of identification. When men place it in a ring and press into a daub of melted wax upon official documents, the signet is a means of affixing a mark of authority or the approval of the one to whom it belongs. It is the means of marking as with a signature by one with the power to rule and affect change. But the signet to which the bride now refers is another of the places in the Song which becomes hard to believe when we begin to understand.

In the history of Israel, the priests were those who stood before the altar of Jehovah offering the sacrifices which would cover the sins of the people. They were not set in place as men to minister to men, but as those who would represent men before God. The people's offerings were brought before God in humble recognition of His holiness, and their need of His mercy and forgiveness. The priests were set apart from the people for the office of priesthood; ceremonially sanctified by the blood of an unblemished lamb, washed, and then clothed in garments designed by God Himself - all for the purpose of gaining entrance into His presence.

The point of the design and materials of the tabernacle; the priesthood with their ceremonial washings and garments; the offerings and sacrifices is explained in these few words found in Exodus 25:8 (NKJV), "Let them make Me a sanctuary, that I may dwell among them."

The heartbreak of Adam and Eve's disobedience caused sorrow to enter the realms of men, but the sorrow experienced by men is less than half of the story. We can never know how much pain God has carried all of these long years by separation from His beloved ones. But we can glimpse His determination for restored oneness through the images which point to our Savior throughout time.

The sanctuary, or dwelling place, God showed to Moses on the mountain included the anointing of a high priest to carry the offerings of the people before His presence. This man was the point of connection between God and mankind.

The garments of the high priest were intricately woven of a specific design. They were made of linen woven with blue, purple, scarlet, and gold threads. Among his garments, the priest wore a breastplate with twelve engraved jewels representing each of the twelve tribes of Israel, and onyx stones upon each shoulder, also engraved with the names of the tribes. Thus, when the priest entered the presence of the Lord, he carried the people with him before the Lord.

In the days of worship in the tabernacle and later in the temple in Jerusalem, the priests were all descendants of the tribe of Levi. But the prophets spoke of one who was to come who would serve as a priest before God, who was also the rightful King. This priest would be as Melchizedek who received Abraham's offering; as one having honor and authority beyond that of the Levites. The writer to the Hebrews in the New Testament clearly shows this priest as Jesus, our Lord.

The prophet, Zechariah, saw Him and described Him this way, "Behold the Man whose name is The Branch! From His place He shall branch out, and He shall build the temple of the Lord; Yes, He shall build the temple of the Lord. He shall bear the glory, and shall sit and rule on His throne; so He shall be a priest on His throne, and the counsel of peace shall be between them both" (Zechariah 6:12-13, NKJV).

"He shall build the temple . . ." Build is "banah;" it is the same word God used to describe how He formed the woman in Genesis 2:22. The woman is the bride, the temple, the habitation of the Lord.

The desire of God for a dwelling place with His beloved found an answer in The Branch who said, "Upon this rock" (the truth Peter stated that He is the Christ, the Son of the Living God) "I will build My church" (Matthew 16:18).

In Him alone is found a meeting place of peace between the justice and mercy of God, between the priesthood and the throne of the King. It is in this the bride now places all her hope and dependence when she says, "Set me as a seal upon your heart, as a seal upon your arm" (Song 8:6).

Life calls to us, draws us, like the sunlight on a stormy day. We search for it, revel in it – this Life. Do you remember my locust blossoms? How as a child I smelled their scent, unaware that it was coming from the trees in bloom? God is like that. He surrounds us with the life that is in Him. If He were to withdraw from us, we would cease to be. But He is generous in His giving. He supplies the air and water and sunlight. He supplies love and laughter and delight to us in the creation He made for us to enjoy; and which reveals what He is like.

Life calls us to Himself, and one day we each will stand before Him and see His face.

We are told a man cannot look upon the face of God and live. Yet we are called to seek His face. How is this? If to look into His face is death to us, how are we to seek His face?

Is the blood of lambs and bulls enough to atone for sin, that we might enter the presence of the One who is Life? Israel came before Him with their offerings, yet the veil separated them from the most holy place where He dwelt. On one day each year, the high priest entered behind the veil alone. When he did, he came with the blood of a bull to sprinkle upon the mercy seat; and when he came before the presence of God, he carried all of Israel upon his shoulders and over his heart. In Jesus' sacrifice, this has been fulfilled.

Jesus takes us with Him into the presence of our Father. He carries us upon His shoulder and upon His heart. He is our priest, chosen from among men, who brought His own blood as the offering for our sin and applied it to the mercy seat – the place where God gets to fulfill His desire to dwell with His beloved.

When Jesus died, the veil that separated us from the presence of God was torn from top to bottom. Jesus breathed His last with these words: "It is finished." The blood of the sacrifice fell upon the mercy seat, and the way into the holiest was secured for those who come before the Eternal One, fixed as a jewel upon the breast and shoulder of our Advocate, our High Priest.

My name is engraved as a seal upon the heart of my Lord. My name is found upon His shoulder. He carries me always in His strength and in His love. Not death, nor hell, nor tempest in life can separate me from the love and might of Him. I am kept because He keeps me. I am kept not through what I deserve, but through what He did.

His love took Him to hell and back for me. His "love is as strong as death." His passion is as unrelenting as the grave. Think about it. What is more final to us than death and the grave? To what do we attribute more power over our lives? Yet the love of God for us is a passionate fire which burns hotter than the fires of hell.

"A most vehement flame" is literally: "a flame of Yah" (Yah – His name; I Am). The Fire of God burns for us. There is no quenching this fire.

". . . The enemy has come in like a flood . . ." (Isaiah 59:19, NKJV), but God Himself fought for us. ". . . And the floods of ungodliness made us afraid . . ." (Psalm 18:4, NKJV), but Jesus gave His very life for us, "all the wealth of his house," (Song 8:7) and counts us worthy of the sacrifice.

> "Set me as a seal upon your heart, as a seal upon your arm; for
>   love is as strong as death, jealousy as cruel as the grave; its
>   flames are a flame of fire, a most vehement flame" (Song 8:6).

The bride is saying, "Nothing is stronger than your love for me. Nothing can separate me from you. To you I entrust my life; all that I am and ever will be."

> "Many waters cannot quench love, nor can the floods drown it.
>   If a man would give for love all of the wealth of his house,
>   it would be utterly despised" (Song 8:7).

The bridegroom answers, "This is my promise to you; nothing will quench my love for you. It can never be extinguished nor diminished in any way, for the flame that burns in my heart for you is fueled by the fire of Infinite Love."

THE POWER OF LOVE

"We have a little sister, and she has no breasts.
What shall we do for our sister in the day
when she is spoken for?" (Song 8:8).

The bride says, "*We* have a little sister . . . what shall *we* do for *our* sister?" The couple is joined in heart and purpose. She knows her concerns are his, and his concerns have become hers. It doesn't matter whose sister she was by birth; she is now their sister, and her need is a shared concern.

"She has no breasts." She is immature. She has an undeveloped, perhaps even an unawakened faith. The question is: how are we to help her prepare for her wedding day?

"If she is a wall, we will build upon her a
battlement of silver; and if she is a door, we will
enclose her with boards of cedar" (Song 8:9).

The bridegroom answers that what we do for her depends upon her needs. Then he draws two scenarios. We need to discover whether she is a wall, or a door. If she is a wall – firm in a stable foundation – we can build upon her. But if she is a door – swinging back and forth upon a hinge – she will need those who are willing to stand alongside her and offer their strength by enclosing her in boards of cedar, until she becomes strong.

The imagery has once again turned toward the picture of the bride as a house or a city; people coming together to form a dwelling place for God. Is our little sister a wall or a door? If she is a wall, we get to teach her how to become an instrument of redemption. We will build upon her a battlement of silver, and she will become a grace-filled force to advance the kingdom of God through sharing the mercy that has been shown to her. But if she is a door, unsure of what she believes or even wants to believe, she will need us to come alongside her and give her the strength and protection of our faith.

I once had a vision I think will help us to understand the intent of this picture. I saw the church, the people of God, marching together as an army advancing in a battle. I saw myself both within the ranks, and able to look on and view the scene from the outside. As the army of God advanced, arrows hailed down upon us from an unseen enemy.

Then I noticed many of us were carrying large silver shields. Each shield was the height of the person carrying it. When the arrows began to pour out on the army, those who were carrying the shields lifted them above their heads as they would an umbrella. The shields fitted together above our heads like the links of a suit of armor. The arrows were not able to penetrate the shields; and although they continued to rain down upon us, they hit the shields and were turned aside, unable to cause harm.

With our shields raised against the onslaught, the army marched beneath what appeared to be an impenetrable silver sea. Yet beneath our protecting umbrella, I looked around and saw there were many within our ranks who had no shield. These were either the very young, or the infirm or wounded. They had no shield of their own, yet they were covered and protected by the shields of others. As we moved along, I noticed we moved at a pace that allowed the young and feeble to stay within our ranks. There was among us the sense of a common and deeply held commitment to leave no one behind.

While the arrows continued to rain above our heads, beneath the shields there was a city of people committed to helping one another. Those who were unable to walk were carried or supported by others. Those who were hurt or wounded were given care and nurture. As long as the silver shields remained in place, none of the arrows could get through; but if ever there was a shift or a gap in the protection we held against the enemy's arrows, someone would be struck and hurt by the unrelenting attack upon our ranks.

I did not see us fighting the enemy with weapons of our own. It was enough that we were advancing, unharmed beneath our silver shields. By this advance, we were reclaiming ground and increasing our ranks as we added to our numbers those we came upon as we moved forward upon the land.

Shall I tell you what I have come to understand by way of this vision? The shields represent selfless love. This is the love against which the accuser of the brethren has no power. It is the love held by those described in Revelation 12:11 (NKJV), "They overcame him (the accuser) by the blood of the Lamb and by the word of their testimony, and they did not love their lives to the death."

The arrows are the unceasing assault brought against the beloved of the Lord by the enemy of our souls. This assault takes the form of a constant barrage of accusing words, thoughts, and even unconscious feelings, which assail us to get us to turn back from our agreement with Selfless Love. Jesus embodies selfless love. When we entrust our hearts to Him as the bride has learned to do, we enter into agreement with the One who loved not His life to the death.

Those who enter this place in Him find there is nothing of ourselves we must fight for; He has fought for us. There is nothing we must protect; He is our protector. There is nothing outside of Him worth gaining and nothing to grasp after; He gives us all that He is. Where He goes, we want to be. He inhabits the air of selflessness; and because we want to be always in His company, we learn to go with Him there.

This is a dimension unknown to our enemy. His whole kingdom is built upon selfishness. No one needs an explanation of selfishness. It surrounds us in this world. It fills the atmosphere and begins to have its effect on human souls in our infancy; the first time we begin to assert our wills. This is where the battle is fought - in our wills.

It belongs to us to choose, every moment of every day, whether we will raise our shield of selfless love and extend the grace to others that has been so freely given to us. The temptation to pull back, to protect or cover ourselves, will leave us unprotected. We can only arrive at maturity by arriving together, of one heart and mind.

Those who are established in redemption's grace (a wall) can be built upon as one who carries a shield and advances the kingdom of heaven among men. Those who are weak, injured, or young (a door) need the strength of others to stand alongside them in the gentleness of our Savior. We must learn that in the atmosphere of heaven, it is counted the greatest privilege to serve another. Our God so loved, that He gave; and we have the joy of going with Him there.

The bride has come to understand what is in the heart of her bridegroom and responds with these words, "I am a wall, and my breasts like towers; then I became in his eyes as one who found peace" (Song 8:10).

Even as we would say to our Bridegroom, "You have established me in your goodness as a jewel in its setting. I see what you want of me; that I would extend to others the mercy you have shown to me. I groan within myself; my heart reaches to agree with you even as towers reach toward the sky. Yes, I want to be with you in this place of self-lessness, but I grieve for I am sure it will not be found in me.

"Yet in the midst of my groaning, I find comfort in your eyes – for I see compassion there. Then I understand: you are the Selfless One! The love is all your own. You will take me with you. You will give me what I need. When my heart is yours, your grace is mine. In this I find all I need."

FRUITFUL IN TUMULT

"Solomon had a vineyard at Baal Hamon:
he leased the vineyard to keepers;
everyone was to bring for its fruit
a thousand silver coins" (Song 8:11).

Baal Hamon literally means "lord of the tumult." It's a fitting description for the world, don't you think? Do you recall that when King Ahasuerus in the book of Esther handed his signet ring to Haman, the enemy of the Hebrews, confusion came upon the land? By contrast, when the ring was given to Mordecai, the land was filled with peace? Wherever evil rules, there is confusion and fear.

In this land where tumult fills the atmosphere, the King, whose name is Peace, had a vineyard. A vineyard throughout Scripture is always a picture of life lived in the spirit. Like the perfect lily amidst the thorns, this vineyard is found in a place desolated by evil; Baal Hamon.

"He leased the vineyard to keepers." He commissioned trusted servants to care for his vineyard and assure its fruitfulness, and he looked for great fruitfulness from his vineyard. "Everyone was to bring for its fruit a thousand silver coins."

If you will recall, I see a thousand as an idiom for holiness as it is ten (which speaks of righteousness or justice) to the third power (signifying God's own goodness). The third power – three: the number for the triune God. Silver is the precious metal which always points toward our redemption. It represents the currency which was used to release us from slavery to sin.

The King expects to find holiness – His own likeness – in the hearts of those who draw their lives from the Vine. "Everyone was to bring a thousand silver coins." It is reasonable to expect the branches of the vine to produce what is in the vine. Jesus made it clear that He is the vine and we are the branches. He is not surprised by the fruit we produce as His life flows through us. What is in Him is what He looks for in us.

The bride is delighted to discover she can give to him what he intended. She says, "My own vineyard is before me. You, O Solomon, may have a thousand, and those who tend its fruit two hundred" (Song 8:12).

The one, who at the beginning of her journey confessed, "My brothers made me keeper of the vineyards, but my own vineyard I have not kept," now has the joy of bringing to her beloved all that he desires, as well as an overflow to supply the needs of those who care for her.

The bride has learned that the life of the branch is found in the vine; and through the vine, life flows in such abundance that its supply works in her like it did upon the fish and loaves of the little boy's lunch. After feeding a multitude, the disciples filled twelve baskets with the overflow.

Here is something I ponder. We live our lives by measure: time, distance, age, weight, fullness. By measure we attempt to ensure there will be enough, and we worry when we anticipate a shortage. But we have before us an open door into the Infinite One. He who holds the seas in the palm of His hand, He who measures the galaxies by the span of His hand, has opened a way before us into life in Him; a life which is marked by infinite abundance.

Infinite abundance surrounds us, like the air which touches our skin and fills our lungs. We may recognize His generous nature; but the question remains: how are we to enter there?

We each are a vineyard planted in a place which is ruled by one called lord of the tumult. We once lived our lives as the tumult directed. We were cared for or rejected, admired or hated, within the atmosphere of selfishness. We took from that atmosphere cues for our behavior. We learned to fight for ourselves so we would have enough. We learned to protect where we could not fight. We learned to be afraid. In this atmosphere, we often suffered lack, pain, loss, indignity, and shame.

But one day a breath of air touched us. It was different from the atmosphere we had known. We sensed it as it brushed by, but it was fleeting, and we were afraid to follow it to where we could not see. But another day it came again; and each time it came, it seemed to whisper our name; and within us was awakened a hunger we could not deny. So we followed, without knowing what.

Then the breath took on a form, and we began to see the likeness of a person. A desire to know him began to grow within us. But we saw and understood so little, and were still so filled with fear. We would follow a little while, then dart away and continue in the life we had formerly known. But there was something wonderful in this person we were beginning to see, something which kept us wanting more.

One day He turned and we saw His face. Then we began to find a direction for the longing in our hearts. It was the day we called to Him; but how little we understood then that this day had come long after He first began to call to us.

This was the beginning of our journey. For each of us, the stories are as varied as the prints of our fingers; yet it is the truth which helps us on our way, running like a golden thread through our lives, and forming a bond between us which gives us the strength of fellowship. While we remain on this side of heaven, we live in a world filled with tumult; yet we are the vineyard of the King of Shalom, the One in whom well-being is found.

As His vineyard, we get to offer to Him a constant supply of the life which originates in Him. We do not bring what we are able. We offer what He is in us. Engulfed in the fire of Infinite Love, we are His in every moment, and with every breath. This is the way we present ourselves to be made holy – through His life in us. As Paul says, "It is our reasonable service" (Romans 12:1).

My vineyard is before me. you, O Lord, may have all that is within me; all that your death and life have won; a thousand silver coins, even your beauty. But this is not all that your life supplies. There is more; two hundred for those who tend the fruit. When I give all to you, there will always be an overflow, enough to give away.

MANY GARDENS, ONE VOICE

The bridegroom now entreats his bride with these words, "You who dwell in the gardens, the companions listen for your voice – let me hear it!" (Song 8:13).

The bridegroom had previously stated, "A garden enclosed is my sister, my spouse." Eve was formed in the garden. Woman/the bride/the habitation of the Lord dwells in the garden. The word for "to dwell" also means: to abide, to settle, or to marry. Here he says, "You who dwell in the gardens." Gardens - plural; there are many gardens.

One day the Lord spoke to my heart, saying, "Pray for the emerging bride." Then He showed me a woman – a bride – rising up and expanding in stature, until she stood strong and beautiful. As she arose, rigid pieces of broken structures fell off her body. She had been inside many different structures, but they had all become too small for her. She could not be contained within them any longer. As each member came forth from the place they had been, they came together and arose as one. She stood and became a bride, as tall as the sky, lovely in form, straight in stature, both confident and gentle in her nature.

The members of the bride are like the jewels on the high priest's breast. There are many; each engraved with one name, each unique, individual, beautiful within itself and having value all its own; yet together, they make the breastplate which covers the heart of the high priest.

I used to think the Lord would be most pleased by me if I were to become invisible. I made it a prayer that I would become like the air, in no way hindering the beauty of His light through my life. But one day, as I began to repeat my prayer to become invisible, Holy Spirit stopped me mid-sentence, "Christy, did I ask you to pray this way? Do you not understand I formed you to reveal My beauty in the unique way that only you can? You are like a jewel, precious in My sight, and through you My light refracts in ways only you can bring."

I learned that day; God does not make us to lose us. He makes us in such a way as to share Himself with us each in our uniqueness. But there is more. As light shines into a fine jewel, the jewel cannot keep the light inside itself. Its very transparency causes the light to spill out in beautiful colors; shimmering as the rainbow around the throne of the One who holds us close to His heart. He is the light. We are His jewels, each one revealing the beauty of His heart.

We each dwell within our own garden with Him. There we learn to hear His voice. We lay down our troubles and learn to rest. We share the delights of loving and being loved by Him, and we learn to trust Him like no other. There are many gardens; for it is in the heart of the individual that God first longs to dwell. But there is one bride with one voice for which He strains to hear.

"The companions listen for your voice. Let me hear it." The bride is formed (built together) of many individuals who speak giving voice to one sound. The companions, along with the bridegroom, strain to hear the sound of the bride. The companions are those who are in the presence of the bridegroom; the angelic hosts, and the believers who have gone before us and now surround His throne. But what is the sound all of heaven strains to hear?

It is the song the bride alone can sing. She sings it back to her bridegroom with these words, "Make haste, my beloved, and be like a gazelle or a young stag on the mountains of spices" (Song 8:14).

THE SONG OF THE BRIDE

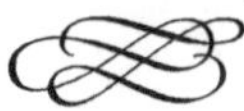

On the day before Thanksgiving, my husband and I, along with our children, were traveling to spend the holiday with my parents. Our way took us through three of the largest cities in our state. The weather was stormy with wind and heavy rain, causing poor visibility. The traffic was often dense; moving nearly bumper to bumper at freeway speeds. The semi-trucks passing by sent blinding sprays upon the windshield against which our wipers were a poor defense.

I am not fond of traveling at high speeds and especially not in crowds. On this trip, I was particularly nervous with the combined conditions of traffic and weather. I trust my husband's driving, but I found I needed help to stay calm. So I asked the Lord, "Will we be okay? Will we make it safely to my parents?" Immediately, I saw us having arrived there, safe and sound.

I felt Him smile as He gave me this picture, and the words, "I know the end from the beginning," came into my heart. The rest of the trip was no more frightening to me than it would be to watch the rerun of a suspenseful movie. If you already know the outcome, the journey can be enjoyed.

I share this story with you because there is much yet to happen in the earth; much that could frighten us. But although the world is facing shaking, sifting, and purging through many different agents, these are not judgments upon the bride. The events around us may be distressing and difficult. We may pass through blinding sprays and face dangerous conditions. But through it all, we hold a promise of well-being.

When Jesus gave John the visions which revealed the culmination and finale of the story of creation, He began with these words, "'I am the Alpha and the Omega, *the* Beginning and *the* End,' says the Lord, 'who is and who was and who is to come, the Almighty'" (Revelation 1:8, NKJV).

After showing John many things which are destined to come upon the earth, He finishes with the words, "I am the Alpha and Omega, the First and the Last, the Beginning and the End" (Revelation 22:1, NIV3).

This is our Bridegroom, the one in whom we trust. The events of our lives transpire within His being, and through it all we are kept in Him. We are the joy of His heart.

There is a finish coming to the reign of darkness in the earth which began when Adam first doubted God's goodness and turned over the deed of the earth. The deed has been returned to its rightful Sovereign, the Son of Man; but until all things are complete, we who are His and are alive upon the earth have an important place to fill.

The bride holds a key to the events at the end of the age. There is a sound heaven waits to hear. It is the voice of the bride saying, "Make haste, my beloved and be like a gazelle or a young stag upon the mountains of spices" (Song 8:14).

Mountains speak of the kingdoms of our hearts, while spices point to the fragrance of worship and the sweet scent of communion. Both a gazelle and a stag are animals which are at home upon the mountains.

Early in their journey, the bridegroom invited his bride to join him on the mountains. She watched him come leaping down from the heights while she stood behind her lattice. He called to her, pleading with her to come with him to the secret places in the clefts of the rock. But her fear was stronger than her knowledge of him. She couldn't see how she could go with him. He was much stronger and more capable than she, so she sent him away, calling the mountains Bether, or separation.

Later, the bride journeyed through the darkness to the mountain of myrrh and the hill of frankincense. Her love and her trust, though fragile and small, lead her to the peaks of Lebanon, to the heart of her bridegroom. When the morning sun began to light the landscape and the mists began to burn away, she was astonished at where her tiny faith had taken her. Her bridegroom told her then that she had ravished his heart by the journey she had made in faith. Each precious step, like the links which formed her necklace, was a choice which drew her nearer to him.

As the bride explored the mountain of her bridegroom's love, breathing the air of Lebanon, she began to change. She learned to walk upon the mountains with her bridegroom. She found even the lions and the leopards were subject to her there. Her bridegroom walked with her day by day as he drew her ever deeper into his love; all the while his love was working within her, transforming her from ragged to royal.

Then came the day when she looked around and realized she was sitting in a place of highest honor. "How came this to be?" she wondered, "The honor belongs to the one who brought me here." She wanted to turn the gazes of those who desired to bask in her beauty toward the beautiful one who held her heart. But her question of why they would want to gaze upon her loveliness was answered by her king when he began his description of her at her toes and finished with the curls at the tips of her hair. She was revealed as royal in every aspect of her being. Now transparent before him, and wholly given to her bridegroom, she carries his likeness in all that she is.

Through her association with her king, the bride learned the ways and thoughts of the kingdom. Her bridegroom says of her that her head crowns her like Carmel (the knowledge that the Lord is God) and her hair (her thoughts) are purple (royal).

Every thought, all her energy, is now engaged in loving him in whatever way she is able. This powerful love is a fire within her. She exudes it wherever she goes. Sadly, she discovers some whom she had expected to rejoice in her love, now turn from her. But she finds comfort in the arms of her beloved, and the rejection she experiences only serves to deepen her faith and strengthen her bond with her bridegroom.

The bride seeks solitude in the wilderness with her beloved; and when she next arrives on the scene, she is seen as utterly dependent upon him. People notice her altered appearance; but she is so taken up with her bridegroom she does not take her eyes from him; and it is he who answers the questions which arise.

The bride wants only to be with her bridegroom in whatever way she may. She has discovered to her delight leaning upon him as she does now that she can feel his heart beating and can sense the direction of his desires and thoughts.

Her vulnerability toward him, her trust and transparency, and her utter dependence upon him have given her the ability to move with him in his dance. There is no awkwardness. Every nuance of movement is shared.

She has learned to sing his song, and she brings to the melody her own beautiful harmony. Each breath and phrase, every transition in mood and key, is done in absolute ensemble.

In a dark and godless world, the bride now offers to her King the thing He most desires. He is enthroned within her through the blood of the Savior upon the mercy seat in her heart. Her love and trust have become the incense which offers a resting place for His beauty. Her being has become a place through which His kingdom touches the realms of earth. His light reaches through her in the way a beam of light enters a dark room when a door is opened from a lighted place.

As I prayed for my nation not long ago, I was shown a picture. As if I was looking down from above, I saw thick darkness blanketing the land. When I cried out to God to come, I saw tiny fires spring up across the land. I continued to pray and watch as more fires appeared. When the encroaching darkness was lit from beneath with thousands of unquenchable lights, it dissolved like a mist before the sun.

The prophet Isaiah saw darkness upon the face of the earth and said, "Darkness shall cover the earth and deep darkness the people, but the Lord will arise over you, and His glory will be seen upon you." The people are instructed in the face of this deep darkness to, "Arise, shine; for your light has come! The glory of the Lord is risen upon you . . ." (Isaiah 60:1-2, NKJV).

We are the vineyard of the King of Peace planted in the land of tumult. We have seen and been convinced He is the One "who is and who was and who is to come, the Almighty" (Revelation 1:8b, NKJV).

Every part of our will and strength, heart and mind, is directed toward receiving the constant flow of His life and offering back to Him the fruit of our worship: our lives laid down. These are the mountains of spices where our Beloved makes His home – even our hearts.

There is a song the bride alone can sing; the song which arises from hearts which have known darkness, pain, and loss, but who sing in the freedom of one who is loved. The worship of the emerging bride as she draws together in unity with her Lord is the sound for which the saints and the angels around the throne of heaven incline toward earth and wait to hear.

"Make haste, my beloved," the bride says, "and be like a gazelle or a young stag on the mountains of spices."

Every hill and valley, every thought and word, all my strength and abilities are yours, my King. Let my worship be sweet, our communion complete. Find in my heart your home.

"And the Spirit and the bride say, 'Come!' and let him
who hears say, 'Come!' and let him who thirsts come,
whoever desires, let him take the water of life freely . . . He who
testifies to these things says, 'Surely I am coming quickly.'
Amen. Even so, come, Lord Jesus!" (Revelation 22:17, 20, NKJV).

RESOURCES & REFERENCES

- "Dictionary of Biblical Imagery" editors: Leland Ryken, James C. Wilhoit, Tremper Longman III; by Intervarsity Press.
- "Eerdmans Dictionary of the Bible" edited by David Noel Freedman; Eerdmans Publishing.
- "Eerdmans Handbook to the Bible" edited by David Alexander and Pat Alexander; Eerdmans Publishing.
- "Interpreting the Symbols and Types" by Kevin J. Conner; Published by Bible Temple Publishing.
- Taylor, J. Hudson. *Union and Communion with Christ.* Minneapolis, MN: Bethany House Publishers, 1971.
- Grahame, Kenneth. *The Wind in the Willows.* Dover Publications: Mineola, New York, 1999.
- Carmichael, Amy. *If.* Dohnavur Fellowship. Christian Literature Crusade

NOTES

2. FRAGRANCE

1. Grahame, Kenneth. *The Wind in the Willows.* Mineola, New York, Dover Publications, Inc. 1999, page 59.

19. REST

1. Carmichael, Amy. *If.* Christian Literature Crusade. Fort Washington, Pennsylvania, 1998, page 80.

74. PURPLE HAIR

1. Markham, Edwin. "Ouwitted." Online. 9 April 2023. https://www.poetrynook. com/poem/outwitted.

ABOUT THE AUTHOR

For Christy Hill, the poetry of Song of Songs is alive with wonder. Through decades of study, she has found treasures that lead into the very heartbeat of God. Christy and her husband, Forrest, are parents of five sons and live on the beautiful Oregon coast. Their family has grown to include five amazing daughters and twelve wonderful grandchildren.